Hannah and Martin

Wisdom Editions
Minneapolis

FIRST CALUMET EDITION September 2024
Hannah and Martin: Some Ontological and Moral Puzzles.
Copyright © 2024 by Stephen J. Vicchio. All rights reserved.

No part of this book may be used or reproduced in any manner whatsoever without written permission except in the case of brief quotations used in critical articles and reviews. For information, write to Calumet Editions, 6800 France Ave. S., Suite 370, Minneapolis, MN 55435

10 9 8 7 6 5 4 3 2 1
ISBN: 978-1-962834-22-3

Cover and interior design: Gary Lindberg

Hannah and Martin

Some Ontological and Moral Puzzles

Stephen J. Vicchio, PhD

Minneapolis

This drama is dedicated to my dear friend, Irene Burell, who kept my life together for several years.

Table of Contents

Introduction: 1

Hannah and Martin: Introduction 1

Short Biographies of
Martin Heidegger and Hannah Arendt 11

Hannah and Martin:
Some Ontological and Moral Puzzles 17

Postscript 73

Appendices 81

Appendix A: Interludes
and Narrations of Hannah 83

Appendix B: Notes on Dramatic Techniques 85

Appendix C: An Essay on Grace, Forgiveness
and Creativity in the Plays of Stephen Vicchio 91

Appendix D: A Philosophical Essay
on Human Nature 97

Appendix E: More On Plato's Eternal Forms 113

Appendix F: Thoughts on Aristotle's Ethics 117

Appendix G: Love in Saint Augustine 125

Appendix H: Foreign Words and Phrases 129

About the Author 135

Also by
Stephen J. Vicchio, PhD

PLAYS

The Unnamed Play
Ivan and Adolf: The Last Man in Hell
Executioner's Hill

OTHER WORKS

Hell: A Detailed History of an Idea
Estevanico: The First Black Man in America
Evil in World Religion
*From Vladimir to Vladimir: A History
of Russian-Ukraine Relations*
Hamilton's Religion
Mala'ika: Angels in Islam
Evil and Suffering in the Bible
Muslim Slaves in the Chesapeake 1634–1865
The Akedah, or Sacrifice of Isaac
The Idea of the Demonic

Hannah and Martin:
An Introduction

This is the precept by which I have lived. Prepare for the worst; expect the best; and take what comes.
—Hannah Arendt, *Letters*

Thinking only begins at the point where we have come to know that Reason, glorified for centuries, is the most obstinate adversary to genuine thinking.
—Martin Heidegger, *Being and Time*

Introduction

Hannah and Martin is my fourth play. It was written primarily in 2015 and in 2024. It deals with philosophical themes that have occupied my imagination for the past fifty-five years. By this, I mean issues related to human suffering and, if there is a

God, why he allows so much of it. Other philosophical themes over the years in my dramatic career are about the natures of love, moral responsibility, and the nature and extent of forgiveness and how to distinguish it from vengeance. In fact, many of these themes can be found in *Hannah and Martin*.

I wrote my first play in the early 1970s in my final semester of college. That semester, I took two courses that would greatly effect, and affect, my philosophical career. The first of these was a Russian literature course that included the reading together of writers like Alexander Pushkin, Leo Tolstoy, and Fyodor Dostoyevski, among others.

The other significant course in my final semester of college was Professor Samuel Hay's one-act play writing course that was essentially designed on how to write a one-act play. In fact, the final exam for that course was to turn in a one-act play that the student had been working on all semester. The course ended in early June, and unknown to me, Professor Hay entered my play in the Young American Playwright's Competition that awards the best written one-act play by a college senior annually.

The following September, I received a letter from the Kennedy Center in Washington, D.C. that told me that I shared first prize with a woman named Beth Henley, who has gone on to have a lengthy career as an American playwright, including her work, *Crimes of the Heart*, which later became a movie as well. She has also written screenplays in her career, after moving to Los Angeles. When we shared the award, Ms. Henley was a senior at Southern Methodist University.

The first prize of the competition included $1,000 shared by the two winners and our plays to be performed at the Kennedy Center for a month. My one-act play was called *An Unnamed Play*. It essentially dealt with many of the well-honored conventions of the history of drama from the Greeks on, things like character, plot, perspective, and what Samuel Coleridge called the "willful suspension of disbelief" in 1817, the view that we have to give up our beliefs for a while and engross ourselves in a fiction that is not real.

Over that thirty-day period, one of the plays was performed as a matinee and the other in an evening performance. The order of the performances was switched every day, so each of us had fifteen matinees and fifteen evening performances.

It was not until the 1990s that *An Unnamed Play* would come back to my consciousness. A theatre in Ohio, the Springfield Repertory Theatre, asked me for the rights to stage the play and, of course, I gave it to them and drove to Ohio from Baltimore to attend the opening.

My second play was entitled *Ivan and Adolf: The Last Man in Hell*. It was written in 1989 and published in 1992 by Wipf and Stock Press, in Eugene, Oregon. This play was also connected to that final semester of my college career. In the Russian Literature course, the final book we read was Dostoyevski's *The Brothers*

Karamazov, a murder mystery novel about who murdered the father of the Karamazov clan in Russia. The four sons of the father were all treated as suspects. And it turns out that the third brother named Dmitri was in fact the murderer of their father.

In a pair of the chapters called "Rebellion" and the "Grand Inquisitor" in the Russian novel, the youngest brother named Alyosha, a seminary student of the Russian Orthodox Church, sits with his elder brother Ivan. They sit in a café, drinking tea out of a Samovar and discuss why there is so much evil and suffering in the world. At one point, Ivan blurts out, "If you have to forgive murderers to go to Heaven, I would just as soon turn my ticket back in."

Ivan Karamazov's politics were decidedly in the Leftist direction of what would become the Russian Revolution and he had a great disdain for anything related to God and the Russian Orthodox Church, even though Alyosha was a seminarian of the Church. Ivan was in favor of the elimination of serfdom in Russia that came about in 1861, nineteen years before the writing of the *Brothers Karamazov*.

When I first read the novel in the early 1970s, I told myself one day I will use this scene in some dramatic way. And so, in the later 1980s, I wrote a play with three central characters. Ivan Karamazov, Adolf Hitler, and an African American maid named Sophie, from the ancient Greek, *sophos*, which means wisdom.

It turns out that we also learn late in the play that Sophie is God, even though she acts as a maid for the two men in Hell. The two males are roommates in Hell, and much like Sartre's *No Exit*, the two men become Hell for each other. The central themes of *Ivan and Adolf*, not surprisingly, are suffering and forgiveness, as well as the difference between revenge and forgiveness.

In addition to *No Exit*, I also relied on many other traditional literary and dramatic texts about Hell and what goes on there, such as Dante's *Divine Comedy*, Christopher Marlowe's *Faust*, William Blake's *Marriage of Heaven and Hell*, C. S. Lewis' *Screwtape Letters*, Chuck Palahniuk's *The Damned*, and Neil Gaiman's *The Sandman*, among many others.

When I went to the opening of *Ivan and Adolf* in Ohio, I had agreed to stay after the performance and answer any questions the audience member may have had. In the back of the theatre in the final row an incredibly old African American man stood up, and steadying himself on his cane, he asks," Why did you make God a Black woman?" I looked up at the ceiling, then to the left and right in the theatre and I responded, "Why not?" The elderly man settled his cane on the seat before him, began to clap and then said, "You got that one right!"

My third play is entitled *Executioner's Hill*. It is set in Holland in 1799. At the time, I was a consultant to the Aegon Insurance Company. They had sold life insurance policies to many people before World War Two and did not know what to do with them. "Should you pay the face value of the policy? What about interest? If included, how much interest?" So they hired me to help them to solve their problem since they did not know what to do with the policies. For six summers I met with officials from Aegon and family members of the policy holders to sketch out an agreement for what to do with the policies. So, my job was to work as a referee of sorts. The agreement we hammered out in the Hague became a model or template for other European insurance companies with a similar problem before and after World War II.

At the end of the final summer, both sides finally agreed on the compensation for the life insurance policies. But in the daytime of the summers in Holland, I dutifully worked on that project. In the evenings, however, I had an entirely different project. I stayed in a small town known as Heemskerk. In the library of the Town Center there are records going back to the late eighteenth century about whether the town would give up the axe executioner in favor of the guillotine.

It is interesting that at the time, those Council members in favor of switching to the French contraption, gave the same arguments that many Americans made in the late twentieth century for the idea of lethal injection, such as cost, degree of certainty, and other concerns.

And that topic was a central one for the Dutch Town Council of the town, and in 1799 they passed a provision that the Dutch town in question would convert to the French guillotine that had been in use in France since 1792, during the French Revolution. One of the central issues in *Executioner's Hill* was whether the blood left on the executioner's axe had medicinal and healing powers.

In the notes of the Town Council of Heemskerk, it was also clear that in the late eighteenth century there was an old wife's tale that the blood from the executioners blade could cure diseases, so it was scraped off the blade and stored in special vials in a pub in the town, and they continued this practice well into the 19th century.

There is also, of course, something ironic about the title. If you have ever been to the Netherlands, you know that it is decidedly flat with very few hills. Much of the country is below sea level. At any rate, the play was written in the late 1990s and not published until 2019 by Resource Publications.

This brings us to the drama at hand, *Hannah and Martin*. When I was a graduate student at Yale Divinity School in the mid-1970s, I took a course on Existentialism and two of the reading assignments for the course were sections of Martin Heidegger's *Being and Time* and a book by Hannah Arendt entitled *Totalitarianisms*.

In that course Professor William Jones told the class about the love affair between Hannah and Martin and that ultimately, even though she was a Jew, Hannah forgave Martin for being a Nazi. At the time,

I was astounded by that revelation. So, I tucked it away in 1975, knowing that one day I will make full dramatic use of this discovery. I also wrote my final paper for Professor Jones existentialist class on the two kinds of love in Plato's *Symposium*, and what Hannah Arendt had to say and write about them. In fact, Hannah's Ph.D. dissertation was precisely on that topic. As you shall soon see, that final paper for Professor Jones will play a key role in the drama you are about to read or see.

And here now is that full dramatic use. In the form of this fourth drama, *Hannah and Martin*. It was mostly written in the early 2000s and finally completed in 2024. Like my other dramatic works, it deals with many of the same philosophical issues to be found in my other plays, including the conventions of traditional drama, the nature of being, and the issues of suffering and forgiveness and how it is different from revenge.

In regard to the conventions of the theatre, I have chosen to use Hannah Arendt as a narrator in this drama. That narration comes in the form of a series of interludes, four in all, where Hannah comments on various aspects of her life with Martin Heidegger. She also moves around the theatre and narrates from different places and seats in the theatre. This was a device that I first employed in the *Unnamed Play*.

Another method I have used in this drama is a few first-person characters who have knowledge of Hannah and Martin, such as the waiter and bell boy at the close of this drama, when Hannah and Martin had dinner in the San Remo Hotel in Rome after the end of World War II in the late summer of 1945.

Most importantly, in *Hannah and Martin* the chief philosophical themes in the play are the same ones to which I have devoted my fifty-year career in philosophy. Evil and suffering, forgiveness and retribution, the nature of love and beauty, the nature and extent of being, and what is, and is not, real and morally good.

I hope you enjoy reading, or seeing a dramatic performance of Hannah and Martin, as much as I have had in writing it. It is a complex drama, full of ontological and moral puzzles. Thank you for your interest in the play, but before we go there, however, we will supply short biographies of both Hannah and Martin.

Short Biographies of Martin Heidegger and Hannah Arendt

We make a space inside ourselves so that Being may speak.
—Martin Heidegger

Evil thrives on apathy and cannot exist without it.
—Hannah Arendt

The Life of Martin Heidegger

Martin Heidegger was born on September 26, 1889, in Messkirch, Germany, a city located in the German Schwarzwald or "Black Forest." His father was the Sexton at a Catholic church in the area. Although he grew up in humble beginnings, his obvious intellect propelled him to become one of the great figures of Western philosophy.

Heidegger received his secondary education in the nearby town of Konstanz. In 1913, at the age of twenty-four, he completed his first full-length philosophical work that in translation usually is known as, *The Doctrine of Judgment in Words about Psychology*. In 1915, he completed his habiture thesis, a requirement for any university teaching in Germany. This thesis was on the work of John Duns Scotus (1266–1308), Scottish philosopher and Franciscan friar.

In the next few years, Heidegger spent his time studying classical Protestant theology and texts by Martin Luther, John Calvins and others. This led to a spiritual crisis for the German philosopher where he rejected the Roman Catholicism of his youth. He completed the break with the Catholics by marrying a Lutheran woman, Elfride Petri, in 1917 in the southwest foothills of the Black Forest.

In the early 1920s, Heidegger became the head of the philosophical movement known as phenomenology. The goal of the movement began by Edmund Husserl (1859–1938) whose goal was to describe as exactly as possible the phenomena and structures of consciousness.

In 1923, Heidegger was appointed as an associate professor of philosophy at the University of Marburg. This is where he met Hannah Arendt who was an eighteen-year-old student, and the professor was thirty-five. The two had a love affair that lasted until 1928. In this period of their love affair, Heidegger published his most important work called *Sein und Zeit*, or *Being and Time*, published in 1927. This work earned Heidegger the promotion to full professor.

In this work, Heidegger introduced the notion of what he called *dasein*, which means being there. He employed this concept in order to dismantle traditional Western philosophy from Plato to Immanuel Kant. In *Being and Time*, Heidegger asks: "If Being is predicated in manifold meanings, then what is its leading fundamental meaning? What does being itself mean?"

In 1928, Heidegger accepted a chair of philosophy at Freiburg University, a job that formerly had been held by Edmund Husserl. Heidegger served as the Rector of the university from 1933 until 1934. It was at this time in his life that Heidegger also joined the Nazy Party. He remained a member of Hitler's party until 1945 and the end of World War Two.

After the war, when Martin Heidegger was asked about his participation in the Nazi Party, he said, "He who thinks greatly must also err greatly." Heidegger appears to have understood that his joining of the Nazi Party was a grave, moral mistake.

After the war, as we shall see in the drama before us, Hannah and Martin met one final time at the San Remo Hotel in Rome. They encountered each other in the dining room of the hotel strictly by accident. After spending the night together in the summer of 1945, Hannah forgave her mentor for his Nazi involvement from 1933 until 1945.

It is not clear why Arendt did so. It is clear that something revelatory happened that night. They had some final connection through letters in the early 1950s, but they never saw each other again. Martin Heidegger died on May 26, 1976, in the city of Freiburg im Breisgau.

The Life of Hannah Arendt

Hannah Arendt was born in Hannover, Germany, on October 14, 1906, to a non-practicing Jewish family. She spent her childhood in Hannover, as well as Konigsberg, Prussia, which is now known as Kaliningrad, in Russia. In 1924, she began to study philosophy at the University of Marburg, followed by the University of Freiburg, and then finally at the University of Heidelberg where she received her PhD in 1928.

In 1933, when Heidegger joined the Nazi Party and began to implement Nazi educational policies as the Rector at Freiberg, Hannah Arendt, who was Jewish, was forced to leave Germany so she fled to Paris. She married Heinrich Blucher, also a professor of philosophy in 1940. She and her husband became fugitives from the Nazi Regime, so the couple immigrated to the United States in 1941. In fact, Hannah was naturalized as an American citizen in 1951.

Arendt's first full-time teaching position from 1963 until 1967 was in Chicago. Later, she ended her academic career by teaching at the New School for Social Research in New York City from 1967 until

1975. Arendt's reputation as a social commentator was established by the publication of her 1951 book, *Totalitarianism*, in which she also discusses antisemitism, imperialism, and racism.

Arendt's *Human Condition* was the second of her major works published in 1958. It is a wide-ranging treatment of what Arendt called the Vita Activa, or "Active Life." In this book, she defended the classical ideals of hard work, citizenship, and political action against what she considered to be a debased Western world.

Of her major works, the most controversial was *Eichmann in Jerusalem* published in 1963 and based on her reportage of the trial of the Nazi leader Adolf Eichmann in 1961. Arendt argued that Eichmann was not a moral monster, wicked and depraved. Rather, she claimed the Nazi leader was guilty of "sheer thoughtlessness." In her mind, Eichmann was an ambitious bureaucrat who failed to reflect on the enormity of what he was doing. For Arendt, Adolf Eichmann was the prime example of what she called the "Banality of Evil."

Arendt's refusal to recognize Eichmann as "inwardly evil" prompted many critics to observe that she prompted the fierce denunciations of both Jewish and gentile intellectuals. The controversy was revived four decades after Arendt's death with the publication of Bettina Stangneth's *Eichmann Vor Jerusalem*, or *Eichmann in Jerusalem*, in which the author argued against Arendt's thesis that Eichmann was not a moral monster.

In addition to the meeting of Hannah and Martin in the late summer of 1945—which is spoken about in the drama—the pair resumed contact in 1950, and in subsequent essays, she defended him, stating that his Nazi involvement had been a "mistake," which is often made by great philosophers.

Hannah Arendt spent her final years teaching at the New School for Social Research. She had a heart attack in her Westside apartment in New Yok City on December 2, 1975, and died two days later on December 4, 1975, at the age of sixty-nine.

One irony about the relationship between Hannah and Martin is that although the teacher was the best-known philosopher of the pair, the student was a much better social critic, as well as being much better known in America than was her philosophical mentor.

Hannah and Martin
Some Ontological and Moral Puzzles

Only the mob and the elite can be attracted by the momentum of totalitarianism itself. The masses have to be won by propaganda.
—Hannah Arendt, Totalitarianism

The poet is in the vanguard of a changed conception of Being.
—Martin Heidegger, Being and Time

Act I
Act I, Scene One. Interlude 1

[The time is the present. A sixty-nine-year-old woman, nicely dress, obviously refined and most likely European, enters the stage through a closed center curtain. She moves to Center Stage, where she finds

a wooden folding chair. She seats herself and then squints at the theatre lights aimed at her as if finding her bearings. She spends another minute looking about the theatre and then begins to speak English with a slight German accent.]

HANNAH

Good evening, ladies and gentlemen. It is likely that only a handful of you know anything about me. For one thing, I have never been on television, and this is America, the only way that one becomes famous in this country. I was born in Germany and raised in a Jewish family. I was trained as a philosopher before the Second World War, my area of specialty was ontology, please do not be put off by the word. It comes from the Greek *ontos*, the verb "to be." ontology, then, is the study of being. It is an enterprise begun by Aristotle and has been continued by various great thinkers in the Western World since that time.

Please forgive me. Already I have frightened away some of you with this talk of Greek roots, being, and intellectual history. [*She looks up.*] These lights are strong. [*She shields her eyes and squints, so she can see the audience.*] But I see that some of you are already nodding off. This reminds me of a philosophy class. At least here someone has the temerity to sit in the front row.

And how can I make this interesting for you? Ontology is the study of being. The discipline asks big questions like "Why is there something rather than nothing?" And ontology also involves itself in smaller questions of being some of which are actually related to the theatre. Consider this question. Does Othello murder Desdemona?

It is clear, is it not, that in one sense the answer is yes. Indeed, if you were to attend a production of *Othello* and in the midst of his jealous rage, the Moor comes to his senses and decided to fire Iago from his service, and then with his wife sought what you call in America these days, "couples counseling," would we not be forced to say, "That is not Othello and Desdemona!" That is not William Shakespeare.

If it is genuinely Shakespeare, then Othello must kill Desdemona. But this announcement hardly settles the matter. Suppose the drama plays itself as the bard intended and the Moor suffocates his wife with a throw pillow in Act V, Scene Two. Why is it that the police will not quickly be called to the theatre to arrest Othello? The answer is clear, is it not, the authorities do not take Othello into custody because he is quite simply not real.

All of this raises other interesting questions about drama and the theatre. Why do we laugh and cry at the theatre or while watching what you Americans call a "movie." We laugh and weep at events that are not real. We must play a trick with ourselves when we consider what is real on stage that we know is not. Some, like the British poet Coleridge, in 1817 first called this the "willful suspension of disbelief."

And yet, as Saint Augustine points out, "we find it pleasurable to cry at the theatre." Indeed, we often judge performances at the theatre by the ability to move us to tears. Sadness at the theatre is a kind of pleasure. This brings us to another set of interesting questions about the chair in which I am sitting. [*She rises and examines the chair.*]

This is much like the thousands of wooden, folding chairs in England and Germany on which aspiring students of philosophy sat before the war, listening to the likes of Bertrand Russell. Ludwig Wittgenstein, Karl Jaspers and my mentor, Martin Heidegger. [*Again, she seats herself.*]

Now tell me, what is the ontological status of this chair? Is it real, or is it not? Does Hannah Arendt sit on this chair? What chair would he bring if a stagehand were asked to bring Hannah's chair from the prop room?

This query about the chair leads to a larger question—the issue of my existence. Professor Vicchio, in a very real way, has raised me from the dead and for this I am eternally grateful. This was an immensely powerful act on his part, but not one the good professor can repeat for any of his dead family members and friends.

After raising me from the dead, does the good professor get to have his way with me? Oh no, not in that sense, but I hear the good professor was, what do you Americans call it a "good looker" in his younger days. What I meant by my question is whether Professor Vicchio is obliged to follow the details of my life, both good and bad, pleasurable and not so?

Must the words he puts in my mouth come directly from the sixty-nine years of my life? If the good professor made up some of the dialogue or made surmises about my life, is that morally acceptable? Is it possible to get the characters right and some of the facts wrong? Would it still be the story of Hannah Arendt and Martin Heidegger?

Now I know that this kind of discussion does not go well with most Americans, a culture that only produced one major philosophical school that, oddly enough is called pragmatism.

Unlike the Germans and the French, you are not a philosophical people. You invented instant coffee and cheese that comes out of an aerosol can. If you know of my life at all, you are interested, most likely, in my love affair with my mentor, Martin Heidegger. I died from a heart attack in December of 1975. The funeral director saw that I had a run in my stocking, but he buried me in them anyway. [*She looks at the run in her left stocking.*] See, it is still there. I was buried in this dress and these stockings in December of 1975, next to my husband Heinrich who had died five years earlier. Our bodies are interred in a small cemetery at Bard College where Heinrich taught for many years.

In a moment, I will pick up my folding chair, if it is my chair, and then escape again into the ether. A moment later, the curtain will rise, and I will reappear as a young woman in her late teens as a philosophy student in the classroom of Professor Martin Heidegger. It will be the autumn of 1924. Most of you did not exist at that time.

I would like you to sit back in your ghostly chairs and take careful note of what transpires here.

At the end of this drama, you will have an important moral task. This task is to be found in another area of philosophy, the realm of ethics or moral philosophy.

[She folds the chair and then moves to the same opening of the curtain she entered. Before she exits, she looks over her shoulder and back at the audience.]

But more about your job later. Marburg is waiting or perhaps a Marburg that only exists with a willful suspension of disbelief."

[She exists through the central opening of the curtain.]

Act I, Scene Two.

[The fall of 1924, the University of Marburg, Martin Heidegger's lecture room for his course on the Platonic dialogues. The room is well-appointed, but a small lecture hall was quite common among philosophy classes before World War Two. Martin stands behind a raised platform on which there is a lectern.

He is thirty-five years old, slightly less than medium height, handsome for a philosopher. A fine print of Raphael's School of Athens hangs behind him on the wall. As the curtain raises, Martin is lecturing to ten to twelve philosophy students seated before him on wooden folding chairs, not unlike the ones in scene one. Hannah is seated in the second row. She is eighteen years old, has dark hair and eyes, pretty but not beautiful. She is the only woman in the room.]

MARTIN

For Plato, then, the principal question he wishes to answer in this dialogue of the *Symposium*, is this: "What does the philosopher, the lover of wisdom, have to tell us about the nature of Eros or love?

If Plato is to be believed the answer is a great deal. Plato suggests through his interlocutor Socrates that although all lovers are not philosophers, only philosophers can be the best kind of lovers.

[This comment raises a minor twitter among the students, including Hannah who has a smile on her face.]

But Plato also suggests in Section 209B that love invokes in us all an unconscious memory of an ideal form of beauty, a form of beauty that goes well beyond the worldly. It is the memory of this form of beauty that creates the yearning for the ideal form of love.

[He reads from the "Symposium" that he holds in both hands.]

"We feel a yearning to couple and to beget an imitation of this eternal form of the beautiful."

[Martin looks up from the text.] Well then, is this section clear? Are there any questions about this part of the dialogue?

FIRST MALE STUDENT

Does Plato feel then that it is inevitable that we are ruled by our passions? Do we have no control over our souls in the process of falling in love?

MARTIN

I think that the language you use in asking your question gives you the answer. Perhaps a portion of another of Plato's dialogues will help us.

[He pages through the text until he finds what he is looking for.]

It is called the *Phaedrus*. In it, Plato offers a striking analogy for the soul—one I might add that Dr. Freud from Vienna must have learned in his years of studying in the gymnasium.

Plato describes the soul and its parts as like a chariot, a charioteer, and two horses, one light and the other dark, or a Bay and a Gray as the horse people call those colors.

The darker horse is filled with emotions and passion

much like Freud's id. It is undeterred by reason, the charioteer. The other horse, the light-colored steed, is obedient and follows the rules of society and church. This is Freud's superego.

For Plato, the charioteer is reason and must control the reins of the horses. Thus, the 'I' part of the self. Freud calls it the ego. For the Athenian philosopher Eros has such a strength that it overwhelms reason, our natural instincts become the soul's tyrant.

Plato has Socrates tell us in his *Republic* that a tyrant is nothing more than "one who has fallen in love with power." It is precisely because erotic desires are not always accompanied by reason that they must be treated with the utmost of caution. For Plato, when Eros is unleashed in an immoderate person the soul is held in the grip of sensual pleasure, the love of money, power, and many other things in life.

HANNAH

[*Who raises her hand to ask a question. Martin points to her.*] [*Very hesitantly.*] Herr Doctor Heidegger, do you think we are all accustomed to thinking this way in this modern age to think of love in such psychological terms?

MARTIN

Your name?

HANNAH

Excuse me sir.

MARTIN

What is your name?

HANNAH

Hannah, sir… Hannah Arendt.

MARTIN

Miss Arendt, I think there is a difference between what is and what ought to be. Plato is speaking here of the most ideal, the most fulfilling kind of love. Modern man often closes his reason off from the rest of his being, I think the result then is a kind of inauthentic life. What is always present in unsuccessful people is a lack of a certain kind of character traits that Plato and his student, Aristotle refer to as moral virtues.

HANNAH

[*She raises her hand again.*] Herr Doctor, why do you suppose that Plato reserves the most refined and authentic kind of love for the mouth of the only female character in the *Symposium*?

MARTIN

Ah yes, Diotima. That is an interesting question, Miss Arendt. [*He looks at his watch.*] At any rate, *tempus fugit*, time flies and we must wait for Plato's next installment. Could you please read Sections 210 to 216 for the next time?

[Hannah feels cut off. Martin gathers up his lecture materials, leaning behind a notebook on the lectern.]

Act I, Scene Three.

[The university study of Martin Heidegger. He sits at his desk and appears to be searching for something in and on his desk and book bag. Outside can be heard the sound of thunder and heavy rain. As the scene opens, a light rapping can be heard on the study window [Stage Left]. At first Martin does not seem to hear it, but after a second and third rapping. He moves first to the window and motions the visitor to the door next to the window. Hannah enters through the study door, [SL.] She is wearing a rain slicker and matching yellow hat pulled tightly on her head.]

MARTIN

Miss Arendt, what brings you out in such weather?

HANNAH

I am sorry Dr. Heidegger; you left this book on the lectern after yesterday's lecture. [*She pulls the Greek text of Plato's dialogues from her inside slicker pocket.*] I was worried that you might need it to prepare next week's Lecture. Forgive me, I noticed it is the Greek text of Plato.

MARTIN

Yes, I feared that I had lost it. I have spent most of this evening searching for it. My parish priest, a friend of the family gave it to me when I entered the seminary at the age of twenty, in 1909. It is not just the book itself, it is also the notes I have written in it over the years. It has a certain sentimental value. It is not something that can be replaced. Thank you... thank you so much., Miss Arendt.

HANNAH

We did the Greek text of the *Symposium* at my gymnasium. I found it particularly difficult.

MARTIN

Plato's Greek is always difficult much more so than his student, Aristotle.

HANNAH

Well I shall be going. My errand is accomplished.

MARTIN

Thank you for playing the role of the good Samaritan. [*Now more softly.*] I was just about to brew a cup of tea. A colleague has brought me back from England this wonderful kettle. Except for Mr. Russell, they are not particularly good at philosophy, but they are advanced in the art of boiling water. Perhaps you would like to share a cup of tea. It is the least I could do after you have gotten wet to the bone on my behalf. Maybe I can now warm you up with a cup of tea?

HANNAH

Yes, yes, I would like that. [*She removes her slicker and hat and placed them on the clothes tree in the corner of the study by the door she entered.*] [*SL.*]

MARTIN

Won't you be seated please?

[As he prepares the tea, Hannah looks around the room that includes wall to wall bookcases and books.]

HANNAH

Have you read all these books?

MARTIN

I am afraid to say I have, some more thoroughly than others. These books are no different than a plumber's tools or a seamstress' needles and thread. [*He gestures around the room.*] They are simply the tools of my trade. [*Martin brings the tea on a tray to a glass table in the center of the room between two stuffed leather chairs. Martin sits in one chair, Hannah in the other.*] Well then, how are you enjoying our reading of the *Symposium* together?

HANNAH

Very much, but I must admit to having some confusion about the dialogue.

MARTIN

I see, and what might they be?

HANNAH

Oh no, Dr. Heidegger, it was my intention to drop off the book, not to impose upon you. I did not come here to interrupt your work.

MARTIN

This is my work. I am here to help my students in any way I can, particularly the good ones.

HANNAH

Well… Plato seems to suggest that there are two distinct kinds of love. In the one kind, the soul becomes the slave to the passions and in the other where reason rules the soul and where one sees in the beloved an imitation of the eternal forms of love and the beautiful.

MARTIN

Yes, that's right.

HANNAH

Well how does one know when she is experiencing one kind of love or the other? Does one's heart beat faster? Are one's palms sweatier? Can we not easily mistake the one kind of love for the other?

[*Martin is a bit taken aback by the question.*]

HANNAH

How does one know if it is the foolish kind of love, the kind that hurtles headlong into the dark, or the kind that embraces the light of eternal beauty?

MARTIN

Perhaps it comes with experience. Perhaps the lover who has become acquainted with the eternal form of beauty in his or her soul can never again mistake one kind of love from the baser kind. Perhaps it lifts a lover to a realm that goes beyond the mundane… A realm that can only be called, as Plato says, is *aionis*, or "eternal." He experienced this eternal beauty in the face of another.

HANNAH

Have you ever experienced this kind of love, Professor?

[She realizes immediately that she has overstepped her bounds. An invisible line that should not be crossed, or what appeared to be an invisible line.]

HANNAH

Please forgive Herr Doctor. I have spoken out of turn. I really must be getting back. I have a great deal of studying to do.

[She rises quickly and moves toward her slicker and hat.]

HANNAH

Thank you for the tea, I very much enjoyed it. *[She moves to the door.]* Please forgive me Dr. Heidegger.

MARTIN

There is no reason to apologize. You have been an angel of mercy. I should apologize to you. My own forgetfulness has brought you out in this terrible weather.

[She moves to the door, stops, and then looks back.]

MARTIN

No, I cannot say that I have experienced the eternal form of beauty in the face of another. I think your question about the two types of love is a great one, perhaps we should take it up in class.

HANNAH

I would like that. Good night, Herr Doctor.

MARTIN

Good night, Hannah.

[She is startled that Martin addresses her by her first name. They hesitate a bit too long at the door. She finally exits. Martin moves to his desk where he opens his found book. He stares at the closed-door [Stage Left], as the sound of torrential rain can still be heard.]

[The lights fade to black.]

Act I, Scene Four

[Two days later, the home of Martin and Elfride Heidegger in Marburg. He sits smoking a pipe and reading a newspaper in a well-appointed living room. A clock on the mantle strikes nine. Elfride enters Stage Left, carrying on a silver tray a tea pot and two cups and two saucers. She is thirty-two years old, blonde, sturdy looking, and quite pretty.]

ELFRIDE

The boys have been put to bed. I thought we could have a bit of tea. [*She arranges the tea.*] I was wondering Martin if we might want to take the boys up to the cabin this weekend. You have been working so hard, we hardly see enough of you, we could get some hiking in

MARTIN

We shall see, Elfride. I thought I might go up to the cabin by myself... to get some work done on the book. I am very pleased these days on how it is progressing. But I feel pressed these days. My lectures take up so much of my time. I hardly find a moment to write. Or think for that matter. Elfride, this is the book with which I will make my mark. I finally have something important to say and I am not finding the time to say it. I am going to call it, *Sein und Zeit*, "Being and Time."

ELFRIDE

Perhaps we could do both. I could keep the boys busy during the day while you work and then more in the evening after the boys go to bed.

MARTIN

We shall see.

ELFRIDE

How are your lectures going?

MARTIN

I think they are going very well. On Wednesday afternoon, I have been lecturing on the dialogues of Plato. I think the class is going very well. I am beginning to see all sorts of connections I have not seen before... You would be interested, there is one female student in the class.

ELFRIDE

Is she capable?

MARTIN

Yes, I think quite so. Perhaps the best student in the class.

ELFRIDE

And you are surprised because she is a young woman?

MARTIN

No Elfride, I am not surprised that my best student happens to be a woman. It is rare I see a student this gifted, male or female.

ELFRIDE

What is the young woman's name?

MARTIN

Her name is Arendt, Hannah Arendt. I think she is Bavarian, judging by her accent,

ELFRIDE

Is she Lutheran or Catholic?

MARTIN

I don't know Elfride. She has dark hair and dark expressive eyes.

ELFRIDE

[*Who seems taken aback by the comment.*] Are you sure she is not Jewish?

MARTIN

I think it is quite possible, my dear, why do you ask?

ELFRIDE

You mentioned she was quite outspoken and very bright with dark hair and eyes. I just thought she might be Jewish,

MARTIN

I did not say anything about her being outspoken. Before you seemed very interested in the young woman. Now because you think she might be Jewish, you call her outspoken.

ELFRIDE

I am sorry I offended you. Why is this student so important to you?

MARTIN

She is not. I simply said that she is very philosophically gifted, I am interested in any kind of student with gifts like these.

ELFRIDE

You speak with much excitement about her. I don't think I have ever heard you speak of a student in these terms before.

MARTIN

My dear, you are making far too much of this.

ELFRIDE

Perhaps you are right, I may be making too much of this. I know how hard you are working trying to finish your book. I just think it is odd that under the current political climate of the Bolsheviks that your best student might be a Jew. It is a very good thing that women are now given more opportunities in the university system. But the Jews can be very disruptive influence. I am not trying to stir up trouble, Martin. I just hope your students understand how much you give to them.

[Elfride is clearly flustered. She rises and begins to clear, as Martin returns to his newspaper. Elfride puts down the tray and Martin his newspaper. He rises and gives her a warm and lengthy embrace.]

MARTIN

Perhaps you are right about the cabin. Why don't we take the boys this weekend? We can get an early start on Friday evening. I can work after the boys go to bed and on Sunday.

ELFRIDE

They would like that…so would I.

[They embrace and the lights fade to dark.]

Act I, Scene Five

[A few days later. One week after Scene One. The lecture hall as it was in Scene One. All the seats are occupied as before except Hannah's seat, which is empty. Martin stands at the podium speaking about Plato.]

MARTIN

I had hoped this afternoon to return to Miss Arendt's question about Diotima. Why does Plato put his most refined comments about the most spiritual form of love and beauty in the mouth of Diotima, the only woman in the room of the *Symposium*? [*He stares at Hannah's empty seat.*] Unfortunately, I see that our own Diotima, the only female in the room, has not decided this fine autumn afternoon to grace us with her presence…So gentlemen, the question is yours. Why is it that Plato relies on Diotima to give the fullest account of love in the Sym…

[A loud crash is heard outside the classroom. Enter Hannah Stage Right. She drops her books, retrieves them, bangs into other students' chairs and then settles herself in her own seat.]

MARTIN

Oh Miss Arendt, we are so happy finally to have you with us this afternoon.

HANNAH

Please excuse me, Herr Doctor, I was attending to a personal matter at the Bursar's office.

MARTIN

We were just about to tackle the Diotima problem.

HANNAH

Why sir is Diotima a problem?

MARTIN

I did not mean to say that Diotima was a problem. What I meant is to say that it is problematical that she is the mouthpiece of Socrates and Plato.

HANNAH

Why is that problematical?

MARTIN

I am sorry. I am not making myself clear.

HANNAH

Herr Doctor, if the eternal forms of beauty and love are the same for all of us, and if it is the best part of all our souls that apprehends true love and beauty, then why would it matter if it is the soul of a man or a woman?

MARTIN

Yes, I think Plato would agree. But does he not also say that women by their nature, by their training and inclination are more inclined to have the darker horse, the passionate one, lead the chariot?

HANNAH

You said Ausbildung und Neigung, in German, training and inclination in English.

MARTIN

Yes.

HANNAH

Are they not different things? Perhaps it only appears as though women let their emotions run wild because that is what men train them to do.

MARTIN

Miss Arendt, are there no relevant, essential differences between men and women?

HANNAH

Certainly, there are, but I wonder if they are relevant differences to the "problem" [*She makes air quotes with her two hands.*] at hand. Plato seems very keen on the soul coming to the apprehension of beauty and love through the rational part of the soul, the charioteer, if you will.

MARTIN

Perhaps you are right, Miss Arendt, you have become our Diotima, albeit belatedly. Why then do you suppose that the ancient Greek of Plato's *Symposium*, he refers to the soul in the feminine form, that is, the feminine noun, psyche? Plato, through Socrates, constantly refer to the soul as "she" and "her," or Sie und Sie. Why is that?

HANNAH

I don't know.

MARTIN

Did you know, Miss Arendt, that Diotima is said to have been a real historical figure that prospered in the 440s B.C. Plato did not make her up. She is reported to be the inventor of what today we call platonic love. In Ancient Greece, she was associated with the word *mantis*, from which we get our mania? For the

Greeks *mantis* also meant "seer" and the ability to know the future.

Some say that Diotima predicted the Plague of Athens sometime between 430 and 426 B.C. that killed between 75, 000 and 100,000 people. But whether that prognostication is true is not entirely clear.

What is clear is that her view of *eros* was far more metaphysical and sophisticated than the other participants at the *Symposium*. Perhaps she was privy to a kind of knowledge that the rest of us know nothing about. [*Looking at his watch.*] Perhaps this is an issue we could take up next time. I hope to have your essays graded by then, please place them on my desk on the way out. That will be all for today.

[The students file out of the room. Each places his essay on the lecture hall desk. Hannah lags behind. She approaches Martin. They are the only two left in the room.]

HANNAH

Dr. Heidegger, I am sorry, I am without my essay.

MARTIN

In your haste to get to class today did you forget to bring your essay?

HANNAH

I am sorry about my tardiness. As I said, I had to attend to a personal matter at the Bursar's Office. That same matter has kept me from completing my paper. I wonder if I could have a few more days to finish it?

MARTIN

[*Still a bit miffed.*] Yes, I will give you two more days until Friday. Miss Arendt, you have genuine philosophical gifts. I want to see those in your essay.

HANNAH

Thank you for the extension, Sir. I will have it to you by the end of the day on Friday.

[He seems to soften]

MARTIN

And Diotima, let's try to make it to next week's lecture on time.

HANNAH

Yes, I will.

[The lights fade to dark.]

Act I, Scene Six

[Friday evening, two days later. Martin's university study, as in Scene two. Martin is on the telephone at his desk when the scene opens.]

MARTIN

[*Speaking into the telephone.*] Yes dear, I should finish up here in an hour or two. Yes, I know we were supposed to get an early start. We can still drive up late this evening…the boys will be asleep in the car anyway. Yes, yes, I know Elfride. We will still be there by midnight...Yes, yes, I will...I will be home as soon as I can. [*The sound of a rap at the office window Stage Left.*] There is someone here, I have to go...I don't know. I will see you as soon as I can. [*Martin moves to the window and motions the visitor to the door of the study Stage Left. Enter Hannah through the door with her essay in hand.*] Miss Arendt, it is 7:00 0'clock.

HANNAH

I know it is late, I was wondering if you would still accept my essay, with a reduced grade, of course.

MARTIN

It was due several hours ago.

HANNAH

Please forgive my tardiness. I have been besieged with a host of family problems and I was only today able to concentrate on my essay.

MARTIN

Miss Arendt, we are all "besieged with family problems." You need to start showing more dedication to your work.

HANNAH

I know that, Dr. Heidegger, but these family problems have been most distressing. I know I deserve no special consideration, please forgive my tardiness.

MARTIN

Sit down for a moment. [*He motions her to a chair.*] Please forgive me for asking, but what are these unusual family circumstances?

HANNAH

I don't want to bother you with my troubles.

MARTIN

If there are mitigating circumstances for why your essay is late, I need to know them.

HANNAH

My father died when I was a small girl. A few years later, my mother remarried. Until recently, my stepfather has grudgingly paid my tuition. But on Wednesday morning, I received a message from the Bursar's office that my fees for the term have not been paid.

MARTIN

I see.

HANNAH

I have spent the last two days telephoning back and forth to my home in Bavaria. My stepfather is adamant about it and my poor mother is caught in the middle. [*She seems to soften and reconsider.*] Dr. Heidegger, perhaps this is a mistake. I have imposed on your good graces enough already... Perhaps I should simply go and *Nimm meine Medizin*, or "take my medicine," as they say in English. I have not been all that comfortable with this university life anyway. I seem to ask elementary questions in your lectures all the time.

MARTIN

Actually, I think you are the most philosophically gifted student in the room. Your questions are always insightful. Your comments display a real grasp of the issues that Plato has to offer. Hannah, you are a gifted philosopher.

[She is startled by his use of her first name and Martin's comment. She rises and appears to be out of breath. She moves to the fireplace, placing her left hand on the mantle to settle herself. Her right hand is still grasping her essay.]

MARTIN

Are you ill?

HANNAH

I am just a little dizzy.

[After helping her to the small couch between two chairs, Martin retrieves her a glass of water. Hannah sips.]

HANNAH

I am much better now, thank you.

[She sits up straight and straightens her clothes.]

MARTIN

What did you write about?

HANNAH

Excuse me.

MARTIN

YOUR ESSAY.

[He points to her right hand where the essay is still grasped.]

HANNAH

The two kinds of love, how one may distinguish them.

[He pulls out the handkerchief in his jacket pocket and dabs the perspiration from her brow.]

MARTIN

What did you say?

HANNAH

That the kind that comes from passion is never elevating, that it is essentially an exercise in self-gratification.

[Martin sits next to Hannah on the couch.]

MARTIN

And the other kind of love? To be exact, Augustin speaks of three kinds of love: the a*mor appetitus*, your first variety; the amor creator, or the love of God. This is the kind of love associated with God and the eternal forms. The third variety he calls *dilecto proximi*, or neighborly love, or *caritas*. In your paper, you only speak of the first two varieties of love.

HANNAH

Then how can we distinguish the first two kinds of love? The greatest kind of love is eternal and unbreakable.

[Their faces move closer together.]

MARTIN

Do you think you have ever experienced the eternal kind of love?

HANNAH

Yes.

[They kiss, tenderly at first, and then quite passionately, As the scene fades to black the telephone begins to ring in Martin's study. But he does not answer it.]

[The lights fade to dark.]

Intermission

[During the ten minute intermission, three pieces of German music by the three "German B's—Bach, Beethoven, and Brahms—should be played. For Bach, three minutes of his "Well-Tempered Clavier." For Beethoven, three minutes of his Ninth Symphony. And for Brahms, three minutes of his Symphony Number One in C-minor. For each scene after this, these pieces should be played in the interim.]

Act II

The telling of stories reveals meaning without committing the error of defining it.

—Hannah Arendt, *Totalitarianism*

Man acts as though he were the shaper and master of language, while is fact language remains the master of man.

—Martin Heidegger, *Being and Time.*

Act II, Scene One. Interlude Two

[Hannah is seated in the final row of the theatre in the end seat to the left. She is wearing the dress she had on when she arrived in New York City on May 22, 1941. She remains seated throughout the entire interlude]

HANNAH

I arrived in New York City in this dress on May 22, 1941, to begin a teaching career in the United States. My husband and I received assistance from the Zionist Organization of America and from the local German population that included people like German philosopher and theologian, Paul Tillich who had immigrated to the U.S. in 1933. When we arrived, he was teaching at the Union Theological Seminary in New York City. Union had been affiliated with Columbia University since 1928.

We rented rooms at 317 West 95th Street and my mother, Marie Arendt, joined us there in June of 1941. Before that, I stayed with a family in Winchester, Massachusetts, who helped me work on my English. I stayed there for a month and returned to New York in July.

My first writing project in New York was an article entitled "From the Dreyfus Affair to France Today." I can summarize the story of Alfred Dreyfus by saying that it divided the Third French Republic from 1894 until its resolution in 1906.

The philosophical themes in my Dreyfus article were the same I returned to throughout my career. Being, the difference between vengeance and forgiveness, the nature and extent of moral responsibility. Interesting enough, these are also the same philosophical themes to which Professor Vicchio has devoted his academic life of over fifty years, as well, from what I hear about him.

The Dreyfus Affair came to symbolize modern injustices in the Francophone world. It remains one of the best examples of a complex miscarriage of justice, as well as antisemitism. Most of my article was about that miscarriage of justice and antisemitism. While I was writing the article, I was searching for a job in New York City, finally finding one at the New School for Social Research., where I taught from 1967 until my death in 1975. I was also the first woman at Princeton to be named a full professor, and I also had teaching posts at the University of Chicago, University of California at Berkeley. and Wesleyan University.

Along the way, I also got my writing done, producing books, articles, and political essays from 1941 until 1975. This work looked very much like the following scene at the New School in 1968.

[Lights fade to dark.]

Act II, Scene Two

[New School of Social Research. Hannah stands behind a wooden podium lecturing in a room full of undergraduates and graduate students. She is holding in her left hand a copy of Plato's dialogues, the same Bejamin Jowett's translation from Greek to German used by Martin. All the students in the room are men. Hannah is the only woman in the lecture hall from 1968.]

HANNAH

And so I ask you a very simple question, "Why is the best interpretation of what love is in the Symposium come from the only female in the dialogue?

FIRST STUDENT

Perhaps it is because only Diotima understands the role of the passions in love, the darker horse in Plato's analogy.

SECOND STUDENT

[*In response.*] Are you saying that when it comes to love, men only act out of reason and convention, like the lighter horse and the charioteer in Plato's example to explain the soul? And that women act from the darker horse ruled by emotions and passions?

HANNAH

I see Herr Schmidt [*She switches to German*] that you have read Sections 246 to 250 of the 1892 Jowett translation of Plato's Greek into English. Ich sehe, Herr Schmidt, dass Sie die Abschnitte 246 to 250 sehr grundlich gelesen haben. [*She switches back to English.*] For those of you who do not speak German, I was just commenting to Mr. Schmidt that he has read Sections 246 to 250 of Jowett's translation very thoroughly... *schon fur dich*, good for you.

[The lights fade to dark.]

Act II, Scene Three

[The same scene a week later, Hannah at the podium and the students in their same seats as before.]

[Mr. Schmidt raises his hand and Professor Arendt's calls on him.]

MR. SCHMIDT

Professor, have you noticed how much sections 246 to250 are like Sigmund Freud's account of the self in his *Introductory Lectures on Psychoanalysis*? Freud's calls the three parts, id, ego, and superego, but it is really the same idea, is it not? In fact, one might say that Freud's model is far superior to that of the ancient Greek, with his *es, ego, und superwego*.

HANNAH

Ah yes, id, ego, and superego, for those of you who do not know German. Do you really think that Freud's explanation of the self is better than Plato? Do you really think so? Freud's model, like his view of God that he is an infantile neurosis, in deference to Herr Schmidt. is completely materialistic and detached from any inherent meaning. Plato implicitly recognizes the innate religious aspirations of the human soul. For Freud, nothing is real that goes beyond matter and the physical world. For Plato, the soul has spiritual aspirations, and we certainly should recognize them. We see these, for example, in Plato's allegory of the cave in Book VII of his *Republic*.

The allegory begins with prisoners who have lived their entire lives chained inside a cave. Behind the prisoners is a fire and between the fire and the prisoners are people carrying puppets and other objects. These cast shadows on the opposite wall. The prisoners watch these shadows believing they are real, not knowing any better.

Plato then posits that one of the prisoners gets free. He sees the fire and then realizes that the shadows are fake. Then the prisoner sees a stairway that leads to the world above. When he finally exits from the cave he encounters the sun.

Now imagine the freed slave returns to the cave to tell the other prisoners of what he has discovered, and that what they perceived of as reality is actually a kind of fake reality.

MR. SCHMIDT

And why does this remind us of Sigmund Freud's view of the self. My professor.

HANNAH

Do you not see that the psychoanalyst from Vienna was a materialist, only capable of seeing the level of the shadows, the fake level. [*She switches to German in preference to Herr Schmidt.*] the *Schatten und fake level*, or "shadows and fake level." Plato posits a much deeper spiritual reality. What he calls the realm of the eternal forms.

MR. SCHMIDT

How is that?

HANNAH

[*Turning to the section of the* Republic *where Socrates tells his student Glaucon about the spiritual realm.*] The realm that the escaped prisoner finds at the top of the stairs is the spiritual realm. And that is the difference between Plato and Dr. Freud. For Freud, there is no spiritual level to existence in his analysis of the human Soul. That is why he is inferior to the thought of Plato on the matter.

[The lights fade to dark.]

Act III

Act III, Scene One. Interlude 3

[Hannah is seated in the middle seat of the middle row of the theatre. She is dressed in American clothes that she acquired in the 1950s on the upper Westside of New York City. She remains seated the entire scene, as she lectures the audience.]

HANNAH

So, I settled into my upper Westside New York life and took visiting professor ships all over the United States. [*She stands up.*] I bought this dress at Bloomingdale's in 1957. Do you like it? Guess what

I paid for it at that time? Eleven dollars. Of course, a gallon of gasoline in 1957 was twenty-seven cents. I know that the world in which you now live, it is now close to four dollars.

By the Fall of 1967, I had settled into my office at the philosophy department of the New School for Social Research at 66 West 12th Street in Manhattan. I taught there for the next eight years until 1975. My husband Heinrich had died five years earlier on Halloween night, 1970.

In that time, I wrote some of my most important books.

[*Out of a book bag beneath her theatre seat, she retrieves copies of some of these books and she passes them around the audience. These books include* Eichmann in Jerusalem: The Banality of Evil, The Origins of Totalitarianism, The Human Condition, *and* On Violence. *She distributes several copies of all four books to the audience.*]

If you take these books home with you and give them a good read, you will get a good idea of what my thinking was like in my early days at the New School. In the meantime, at the New School, I also lectured and discussed many of these ideas such as those that appear in this lecture from 1967.

[The lights go to dak for a moment and then come back up to reveal the set during Act Three, Scene Two.]

Act III, Scene Two.

[Hannah Arendt at the podium of a classroom at the New School, in the Autumn of 1967. She holds her worn copy of Eichmann in Jerusalem, in her left hand, while she gestures with a pen in her right hand. The notorious Adolf Eichmann had been captured and put on trial in early April of that same year.]

HANNAH

After escaping to Argentina and working in a Mercedez Benz factory there, Oscar Adolf Eichmann was on a bus that stopped near his house in Buenos Aires, Argentina. Two men approached him and said the only three words in Spanish these Israeli intelligence agents knew: "*Un momentito, Senor.*" or "May I have a short moment, Sir?"

This episode happened on May 11, 1960. When Eichmann reluctantly acknowledged the men, the two agents sprang into action, wrestling the Nazi to the ground and then into the back seat of a waiting car. As the car sped away, they tied Eichmann down and covered him with a blanket in the back seat.

I knew about this because I attended his trial and wrote about it for the New Yorker and in my subsequent book, *Eichmann in Jerusalem*. Eichmann spent nine months in prison and then was tried in Jerusalem for crimes against humanity, beginning on April 11, 1961. The trial was held at the Beit Ha'alam Community Center in Jerusalem. Three Israeli judges presided on the Proceedings.

At 8: 57 in the morning on 11th April, 1961, a concealed door in the wall behind the plexi-glass box in which Eichmann would sit, the defendant was ushered into the dock. A ripple rang through the spectators as they began to realize that Oscar Adolf Eichmann had appeared in the courtroom.

Everyone turned to look at the Nazi mastermind.

More than 100 witnesses testified at the fourteen-week trial that ended on December 11, 1961. Eichmann was convicted of 15 counts of crimes against the Jewish people and crimes against humanity. Oscar Adolf Eichmann also was convicted of war crimes and being part of a global criminal organization. [*She looks at the book in her hand*] And I was there to see all of it.

That will be all for today. For the next time, please finish *Eichmann in Jerusalem*, and bring any questions you have to next week's class.

[Lights fade to dark.]

Act III, Scene Three

[A week later in the same classroom of the New School. Hannah holds the same book she had the previous week, as if she is continuing the same narrative.]

HANNAH

At his trial Eichmann told the court he had been a victim in becoming involved in these horrors. But they were not committed willfully. I never wanted to murder anyone. Only the state leadership was guilty of these crimes. I was only "following orders."

Eichmann's attorney appealed to the Israel Supreme Court that ultimately reaffirmed the original verdict on May 29, 1962. Mr. Eichmann was sentenced to hang on June 1, 1962. Eichmann asked for clemency in his final words, but his plea was to no avail.

So, Oscar Adolf Eichmann was hanged in Tel Aviv on May 31, 1962. [*She holds up her book so her students can see the cover.*] And Viking Press published this book a year later in 1963.

The subtitle of the book was *The Banality of Evil*. which became very controversial in Israel and elsewhere. We will discuss this next week in our final class. Don't forget to bring your final term papers that are due next week, as well.

[The lights in the classroom begin to dim until finally they go to dark.]

Act III, Scene Four.

[A week later, Hannah's final week of the term. The students are seated as they were in the previous weeks. Hannah stands behind the lectern, again holding her copy of Eichmann in Jerusalem.]

HANNAH

At the close of last week's lecture, I told you that this book began to be controversial after its publication in 1963. That was primarily the case because of the subtitle—*The Banality of Evil*.

Let me begin by saying that many questions arose about what I meant by that phrase, the banality of evil. So, I will say a great deal in this final class of the term of what I meant, and still mean, by the phrase.

What I meant by the phrase is how common the capacity to do evil can be seen in human nature, an issue, for example, that Saint Augustine dealt with in his *Confessions*, that we read together earlier in the term, and his eating of the pears episode and its relationship to peccatum originale, or "original sin." We have discussed this incident in Book Two of the *Confessions* earlier this term. I have also spoken of this idea of original sin in my book, *The Human Condition*.

At one level what I meant, then, about the "banality of evil" is how commonplace we find human beings doing very evil things.

A second point concerning the phrase the banality of evil is that Adolph Eichmann was more like a clown than a monster. Eichman was entirely incapable of original thought. He was a "joiner" beginning early on in his life and never changed until the day he was hanged, when he still said, "I was just following orders." Because of this, I made the argument in this book that Eichmann lacked the first of Aristotle's famous conditions for full moral responsibility.

As Professor Vicchio will tell you, in his *Ethics*, Aristotle set out four conditions for full moral responsibility. These were: the intention to do evil, the knowledge of right and wrong, the knowledge of the circumstances in a given moral case, and finally, the "ability to do otherwise." That is, to act freely. Now, in this book I make the argument that Eichmann did not meet any of these conditions for full moral responsibility. If he was operating on the Nazi definitions of good and evil, then he lacked the second condition, as well. In his idea of "just following orders" we see that he was unaware of the proper circumstances of his case. And if he was simply following orders, and he was a life-long joiner, then did he have the ability to do anything other than what he did? I think the answer is No.

[A male graduate student in the front row on the left raises his hand to ask a question.]

MALE STUDENT

But during the trial, did Eichmann not say that he was following Immanuel Kant's categorical imperative, "That one should always act as if your action is a categorical imperative, or universal moral duty?

HANNAH

Yes, he did, on three separate occasions. But he reformulated the categorical imperative to meet his own needs. He invoked moral duty to become: Act in such a way that the Fuhrer would want me to act or would himself so act.

In my book, I offered a quick rejoinder to this principle. [*She reads from her text*] "Kant to be sure had never meant anything of the sort; on the contrary, to him every man was a legislator in the moment at hand, by using his "practical reason' man found the moral principles that could and should be the principles of the moral law."

I think it is very possible that like the view of Augustine and Thomas Aquinas, Immanuel Kant thought that we are born with an inherent knowledge of the moral good. It is not something we learn. The Ancient Jews had a belief in what they referred to as the two *Yetzerim* Theory. It was a belief that all humans are born with a *Yetzer Ha Ra*, or "evil inclination," and a *Yetzer Tov*, or a "good inclination." The human will is what the Jews believed puts one or the other into play. I think something like this view was held by both Thomas Aquinas and Immanuel Kant.

Eichmann stated in court that he had always tried to abide by Immanuel Kant's categorical imperative. I argued in this book that Eichmann had taken the wrong lessons from Kant. Eichmann did not recognize the importance of what we call the golden rule, or *goldene regel*, in German. [*When she says this, she looks at Herr Schmidt.*]

I argued that Eichmann did not recognize the principle of reciprocity that is implicit in the Categorical Imperative. He had only understood one's actions as it coincided with the general, Nazi Law.

Finally, there was one other factor that is involved in what I meant by the banality of evil. And that is this. Some critics of the book argued that people like Eichmann were simply insane and could not be fully morally responsible. But there is an unknown fact that is often overlooked related to the life, trial, and execution of Adolf Eichmann. During his imprisonment, before his trial, the Israeli government sent six separate psychiatrists and psychologists to examine the Nazi leader.

These psychological examiners found "no trace of any mental illness or disorder." One doctor remarked that his overall attitude toward his family and other people was highly desirable." Another said that the only unusual trait about Adolf Eichmann was "being more normal in his habits and speech than the average person. He was just following orders.

In a lot of ways, the Nazi resembled the Soviet Union in that as Kruschev once said, "Here is the criminal, now go find the crime." The Nazis already knew that the Jews were a class of criminals. Then they sought to put them out of business or put them in prison or a concentration camp.

I made the same point about Eichmann in my book about him. I wrote "I was struck by the manifest shallowness in the doer, which made it impossible to trace the uncontestable evil of his deeds to any deeper level or roots or motives. The deeds were monstrous, but the doer, at least the very effective one now on trial, was quite ordinary, commonplace, and neither demonic nor monstrous."

Eichmann's shallowness made it impossible for him to go beyond the "Here's the criminal, now go find the crime," much like in your own day with the treatment of Donald Trump. They know he is a criminal, now go find the crime, or in his case, many crimes in many jurisdictions.

Other critics of my *Banality of Evil* thesis included some close friends, including philosopher Gershom Scholem and my writer friend Mary McCarthy. Professor Scholem wrote to me in 1963, after the book had come out. He wrote that "The banality of evil is merely a slogan that does not impress me, certainly not the product of a profound analysis."

When *Eichmann in Jerusalem* was published, my friend Mary McCarthy, who spoke at my funeral, in 1963 wrote me a letter in which she observed: "It seems to me that what you are saying is that Eichmann lacks an inherent human quality, the capacity for human thought, consciousness and conscience. Then is he not simply a monster?"

I think that Mary McCarthy was correct in her interpretation of the *Banality of Evil*. And on that I will bring this class and this term to a close. Please put your term papers on my desk on your way out. Good luck to all of you.

Professor Vicchio has informed me that the criticisms of my book did not end with my death in December of 1975. In fact, philosopher Alan Wolfe in his book, *Political Evil* published in 2011, criticized me for "psychologizing—that is, avoiding—the issue of evil as evil."

Historian Deborah Lipstadt, in the year 2000 and then in her 2011 book, *Eichmann on Trial*, also suggested that my use of the English word "banal," also *banal* in German, was "hopelessly flawed."

These contemporary criticisms were not all in English. German historian Bettina Stangneth wrote a book with a clever title called, *Eichmann Vor Jerusalem*, which is *Eichmann Before Jerusalem* She pointed out that in many interviews with Eichmann while he was in prison, he admitted to having a kind of Jekyll and Hyde dualism. Stangneth's main conclusion was that Eichmann did lots of evil without being evil.

Stangneth, in these interviews, quotes Eichmann this way, "The cautious bureaucrat that was me, yes indeed, but this cautious was attended by a fanatical Nazi warrior, fighting for the freedom of blood, which is my birthright."

Dr. Stangneth also suggested that four months before the Eichmann trial I already had arrived at a conclusion about his character in a letter I wrote to Hans

Jonas on December 2, 1960. In that letter I wrote, "The upcoming trial will afford me the opportunity to study this walking disaster."

The Banality of Evil notion was also criticized by my friend and mentor, Hans Jonas, in a letter he wrote to me when the book came out, criticizing and condemning my use of the phrase. Hans Jonas was a German-born American, Jewish philosopher. He taught at the New School for Social Research from 1955 until 1976, where he was the Alvin Johnson Professor of Philosophy. Jonas was mostly responsible for me getting my teaching position at the New School.

Another criticism of my book came from Professor Gershom Scholem, German-born Israeli philosopher and historian. He claimed that in my Eichmann book, I was lacking in what he called *Ahavat Yisrael*, or love for the Jews.

So, the criticisms of my expression of the banality of evil have continued to the present time. In my defense I might add that I failed to give enough attention to Eichmann as Nazi Warrior. I may indeed have arrived at a conclusion about Herr Eichmann long before his trial. And I did not make enough references to my own people, the European Jews in *Eichmann in Jerusalem*.

And with that, I will bring this class, and this term of my lectures in the autumn of 1968, to a close. Good luck to all of you. I wish you a nice holiday break until next term.

[The students stand up and applaud. Then they file past Hannah and place their term papers on her desk on the way out.]

[The lights fade to dark.]

Act IV

The trouble with lying and deceiving is that their efficiency depends entirely upon a clear notion of the truth that the liar and the deceiver wish to hide.

—Hannah Arendt, *Eichmann in Jerusalem.*

There is no such thing as an empty word, only ones that are worn out and yet still remain true.

—Martin Heidegger, *Being and Time*

Act IV, Scene One. Fourth Interlude

[Hannah sits center stage on the same folding chair she occupied in the beginning of this drama. Again, she wears the dress she wore at her funeral with the same black stockings with the run on the left leg, on December 9, 1975, the day of her funeral.]

HANNAH

I had a heart attack on the morning of December 5,

1975. Curiously enough, I was wearing this dress at the time, and I was buried in this same dress. Do you like it? [*She stands up so the audience can see.*]

Because of the grace of God, and His sending me to Heaven after my death, I was able to see the speakers at my funeral. The three main speakers on that morning were philosophy Professor Hans Jonas, writer and friend, Mary McCarthy, and my publisher at Harcourt Brace, Bruce Jovanovich. Each of them said passionate and laudatory things about me. Dr. Jonas said about me, "She set standards after which no cheap formula on the human predicament will pass muster."

My friend Mary McCarthy began her eulogy of me by saying, "I want to speak of Hannah as a physical being. She was a beautiful woman, alluring, seductive, particularly with her eyes that were brilliant, sparkling, as if rays of great intelligence leaped out of them. But also deep, dark pools of inwardness. There was something unfathomable in Hannah that seemed to lie in the reflective depths of those eyes."

Bill Jovanovich, my publisher and close friend, said about me that morning: She was passionate in the way that believers in justice may become and that believers in mercy must remain. She detested violence but defended disobedience in a just civil cause. She followed wherever serious inquiry would lead her, and if she made enemies, it was never out of fear. As for me, I loved her fiercely.

After the funeral, my body was taken to Hartsdale, New York, where it was cremated at Ferncliff, a farm owned by the Astor family. But this story is not over. I need to take you back to August of 1945, just after the war had ended. when I made one of my final trips back to Europe. In this case it was to Italy at the San Reno Hotel in Rome.

This was the last time Martin and I saw each other. I had booked a room there knowing nothing about what was to follow. I came down from my room on the 11th floor of the San Remo in order to have my supper. When I entered the dining room, there were two men already there, an Italian waiter named Luigi and Professor Martin Heidegger sitting at a table under the only window in the room. I will turn this drama over to Luigi's, who luckily spoke German, commentary of what happens next.

[The lights fade to dark and come back up three minutes later.]

Act IV, Scene Two

[The San Remo Hotel in Rome, one of the oldest long-standing hotels in all of Europe. Hannah had booked a room there in late August of 1945, just after the end of World War II. Hannah is dressed in 1940s American clothes, stylish dress and matching jacket. Hannah enters the dining room of the San Remo. The only two people there when she enters are a waiter, a young Italian man and, at the far end of the din-

ing room, sitting alone under the only window in the room is Professor Martin Heidegger.

The spotlight in the theatre shifts to Center Stage where Hannah has left the stage and been replaced by Luigi, the waiter to record the scene for posterity. He is dressed in a dark jacket with a black bow tie. Luigi delivers his speech from the front steps of the Hotel San Remo.

Luigi speaks in front of a faux prop entrance to the San Remo Hotel.]

LUIGI

When they first met Hannah and Martin shared a long embrace and short kisses on both cheeks, a normal European custom in many parts. They ordered drinks, followed by a three-course meal that included fish and a German white wine. After dinner, they had coffee. The bill was paid by Martin who left me a sizable tip.

From what I could gather, much of the conversation between the two at dinner was about Hannah's Jewishness and Martin's belonging, or *zugenorigheit*, to the Nazi Party that he joined in May of 1933 and continued until 1945 and the end of the war.

She asked him at what point in their time together did he realize that she is Jewish? Or *Wann wussten Sie ich Judin bin?* He responded, *Ich habe es schon sehr fruh in Jahre 1924 geahnt*, or I suspected it very early on sometime in 1924. I gathered that he attained emeritus status in 1953, but he was never allowed to resume his teaching, because of his Nazi associations.

After dinner, the two left the dining room together and were seen getting in the elevator together which was pushed to floor eleven, where Hannah's room was located. A friend of mine named Marco was a bell boy at the San Remo. He was called to the eleventh floor to retrieve the luggage of both Martin and Hannah the following morning. One other thing we know is that after that night at the Hotel San Remo, Hannah publicly forgave her mentor and lover for becoming part of the Third Reich. We do not know what went on in that room on the eleventh floor, but surely it was transformational and somehow full of forgiveness and a lack of Vengeance.

What happened that night on the 11th floor of the San Remo Hotel is anyone's best guess. But for me, that dinner in the dining room of the San Remo Hotel was one of the most thrilling and memorable times of my life.

[The lights fade to black.]

Act IV, Scene Three

[Hannah sits on the same wooden folding chair on which she first appeared in this drama. She is dressed in the same red dress from Act I, Scene One.

She addresses the audience from Center Stage of the theatre.]

HANNAH

Earlier in this drama I told you that in the final scene I will give you a job to do to end this play. We have come to that point. This task I have for you is fairly simple. If you believe that I, Hannah Arendt, was morally correct in forgiving Martin Heidegger, I want you now to stand up. I will tell you that the night on the eleventh floor of the Hotel San Remo Martin and I made love, he was 43 and me 25 and our conversation afterwards that night was so tender and so transforming that Martin became his old self, much like my time with him in university.

I should point out one other fact about Martin that only became known in 2014 when a previously unknown *Black Notebook*, as it was called, came to light. What it revealed is that Martin was preoccupied with what he called the *Welfjudentum*, or "World Judaism." He thought it was "one of the main drivers of Western modernity which he viewed negatively. His personal notebook, then, showed clearly that he had a disdain, and some might say, a hatred of the Jews, his entire academic life. After that night at the San Remo Hotel, Martin and I never saw each other again. We did write a few letters back and forth in the early 1950s, but that was the last of our communications. After the night at the San Remo I also began publicly to express my forgiveness in regard to Martin's Nazi connections from 1933 to 1945. And I continued to do so for the rest of my life.

Through all of that, however, and thanks to Professor Vicchio for informing me of Martin's *Schwarzes Notizbuch* or *Black Notebook*, I remained faithful to my feeling of forgiveness and mercy in regard to Martin Heidegger and had no desire to speak of retribution or vengeance in regard to him.

So, we are at that moment and the close of this drama. If you believe I did the morally right thing of forgiving Martin Heidegger for being a member of the Nazi Party from 1933 until 1945, I want you now to stand up.

[Everyone seated in the audience looked around the room, to see if others stood up from their theatre seats, but no one rose from his or her seat.]

The End

Postscript

In the 1970s I went on a skiing trip with some friends to a home in Colorado. At dinner after the first day of skiing, the dinner conversation turned to the Second World War and the Nazi regime. I was surprised to find and hear a kind of fondness for Hitler and his movement, so much so that I spent the night in a car because of my astonishment at the dinner scene.

Throughout my entire scholarly and teaching careers, I, like Hannah Arendt, spent my time writing about vengeance and forgiveness. Even early on, in the 1970s, I could not imagine that at that time anyone could have positive things to say about Adolf Hitler and his regime.

In my dramatic career, I have stuck to these same themes of evil, suffering, vengeance, and forgiveness. And we see at the end of *Hannah and Martin* I have retained my original scholarly views about the Third Reich and its leader.

I think the fact that no one stands up in the theatre at the end of the drama is a great testimony to the human heart and spirit. Saint Augustine believed in original sin, but he also believed that the human apprehension of the moral good is also something that humans are born with. Earlier in this drama, I suggested that the Ancient Jews with their two *Yetzerim* theory, Augustine, Thomas Aquinas, and Immanuel Kant as I maintained earlier, all believed that the moral good is known inherently and not learned. I surmise that this is the view of the nature of moral goodness held by Hannah Arendt, as well.

This inherent understanding of the moral good, I think, at the end of *Hannah and Martin* is what ruled the souls of the members of the audience. They had a full understanding of the nature of moral goodness. In short, I think they got it morally right, even though all human beings are also capable of doing extraordinary evil.

In some ways this brings us back to the Platonic metaphor for the soul in the *Phaedrus* of the chariot, the charioteer, and the bay and gray horses. The audience in making their decision about the close of the drama were acting with reason and the white horse as their guides. Remember the gray steed are the rules of society and church. They did not seem to be acting with their emotions, passions, and feelings. The audience members, I would argue, acted in unison the way they did in *Hannah and Martin* because they inherently knew that the "crimes against humanity perpetrated against the Jews were simply morally wrong. So, in the end, the audience in the theatre appears to have done the morally right thing. And the author, Professor Vicchio, agrees with them, as I think would have Hannah Arendt, as well.

All the audience members were doing at the close of *Hannah and Martin* was simply following what they all inherently knew to be true. That the violent crimes committed by the Adolf Hitler and his minions were simply morally wrong.

Another way to see the inherent notion of the moral good are the products of research I conducted in the 1990s that compared the responses of grade school children, ages ten and eleven, to college undergraduate students, as well as American police officers about how to respond to a number of moral dilemmas I gave them to solve.

Traditionally in Western philosophy a moral dilemma occurs when two moral values or moral duties collide with each other, so that both cannot be kept at the same time. When the United States decided, for example, to drop the two atomic bombs on the cities of Hiroshima and Nagasaki, they did so understanding that many innocent people would be harmed or killed. Thus, the value "Don't kill or harm innocent people," and the value, "End a war in the simplest way possible," came into conflict with each other and created a moral dilemma.

My father, who fought in World War Two, and myself only had one disagreement that I can remember in our relationship. He was in favor of dropping the bomb, while I was not.

The most interesting result of that research on the three cohorts and moral dilemmas is that the children gave the same answers in regard to the moral dilemmas presented to them, as did the other two adult groups.

There are several ways one might interpret these results, but the one I favor the most is that the three groups gave the same answers to the moral dilemmas, chiefly because they were given their answers in the context of their inherent, in-born understanding of the nature of moral goodness.

In my view, this is the same reason why none of the audience members at the close of *Hannah and Martin* chose to stand up to indicate that Hannah Arendt did the morally right thing.

It was, plain and simple, morally wrong to do so, and our inherent understanding of moral goodness tells us so.

From Hannah Arendt's early days at Hebrew School in Konigsberg in the early 1920s, she must have learned that the first two chapters of the Book of Genesis contain two separate accounts of the creation of human beings. The first of these is Chapter 1:27-31, and the second account occurs at Chapter 2:7. In the first of these God created humans in his "own likeness, male and female He created them." At the close of this account at 1:31, God saw that the making of humans was "very good," where everything else He has made so far was simply good.

In the account of making human beings in chapter two of Genesis, God formed "man from dust and then breathed into his nostrils the breath of life" "and this made the man a living being." Later, in the same book, we are introduced to the idea of the two *Yetzerim* theory, that God made man with two different imaginations or inclinations, the *Yetzer Ha Ra*, or "evil imagination" and the *Yetzer Tov,* or good inclination, which the ancient Jews believed was stronger because humans were made "very good."

From these Genesis texts, we may make the following conclusions. First, that when God made humans, He declared them, by nature, to be very good. And secondly, that God so arranged human nature that its basic goodness, as well as the capacity to do horrendous evil, as well.

By the time we get to the philosophical work of Bishop of Hippo, Augustine, in his two major works, *the City of God* and *The Confessions,* the north-African bishop confirmed his views on Genesis' "very good" nature of humans, as well as their capacity to do heinous evil, which he believed stemmed from what he called *Peccatum Originale*, or "Original Sin." Above all, Augustine was convinced that the idea of moral goodness is something that human beings are born with.

If we fast-forward to the thirteenth century and the work of Italian philosopher Thomas Aquinas, we again find the ideas that humans are born with a natural understanding of the moral good, while also believing in original sin.

By the time we get to German philosopher Immanuel Kant and his theory of the categorical imperative, we find two parallels to the views of Thomas Aquinas. First, that humans are different from the rest of creation because of their capacity to reason, and that humans because of reason, humans are able to comprehend the universal and inherent nature of the moral good.

This brings us back to two philosophical points, Hannah Arendt's understanding of the nature of moral goodness, and secondly, why no one in the audience stands up at the end of "Hannah and Martin." In regard to the first point, Hannah Arendt was steeped in the philosophy of Saint Augustine, so much so that her Ph.D. dissertation in Germany was entitled, *Der Liebesbegriff bei Augustin. Versuch einer philosophischen Interpretation* or *On the concept of love in the thought of Saint Augustine: Attempt at a philosophical interpretation*, also known as *Love and Saint Augustine*.

In a later work called the *Human Condition*, Dr. Arendt again appropriated the basic beliefs in original sin and the inherent understanding of the nature of moral goodness. This brings us to our second philosophical question, that is, why does no one rise from his or her theatre seat when confronted with Professor Arendt's question at the close of the drama.

There may be many different ways to answer her question, and thus to explain the behavior, or lack of behavior, of the audience at the theatre featuring a performance of *Hannah and Martin*, but the simplest one may well be the best one. No one leaves his or her seat at the theatre because each of the audience members know, universally and inherently, that it would be morally wrong to do so.

Appendices

Each of the following Appendices is offered in the hope of providing important information to aid the understanding of the philosophical nature of this drama. To that end, these Appendices consist of the following:

Appendices of Stephen Vicchio's ***Hannah and Martin.***

> Appendix A: Interludes and Narrations of Hannah.
>
> Appendix B: Notes on Dramatic Techniques.
>
> Appendix C: An Essay on Grace, Forgiveness and Creativity in the drama of Stephen Vicchio.
>
> Appendix D: An Essay on Human Nature.
>
> Appendix E: More On Plato's Eternal Forms.

Appendix F: Thoughts on Aristotle's Ethics
Appendix G: Love in Saint Augustine
Appendix H: Foreign Words and Phrases.

Appendix A: Interludes and Narrations of Hannah

In which Hannah is the narrator throughout the drama.

1. Act I, Scene One
2. Act II, Scene One
3. Act III, Scene One
4. Act IV, Scene One

Appendix B:
Notes on Dramatic Techniques

I would prefer to fail with honor than to win by cheating.

—Sophocles, *Letters*.

When the trouble is all done, when the battle is all lost and won.

—William Shakespeare, *Macbeth*.

It is only in drama that the prospects of literature—at least the tragic kind—can truly be seen.

—Hannah Arendt, *Reflections on Literature and Culture*.

Introduction

Since the time of the Greeks, there has exited various dramatic technique in the theatre, as well as many that do not fit the classical mold. Sophocles, Aeschylus, and Euripides are the most significant Greek playwrights who introduced things like character, plot, denouement, and other things.

In the late sixteenth century and early seventeenth century, William Shakespeare also relied heavily on many of these same dramatic elements, but, at the same time he also developed some dramatic techniques that went away from the classical model of drama. For examples, the British poet and playwright introduced the ideas of extended monologues or what are sometimes called soliloquies by individual characters such as in *Hamlet* and *Othello*, for examples. I use the extended monologue technique in the soliloquies of Hannah, as well as the material from the two Italians at the close of the drama. The theme of jealousy in *Othello* is another fine example of this technique.

A second dramatic element that is central to Shakespeare's theatre is the idea of recurring imagery of themes throughout a play, such as the theme of death in *Hamlet*. A third dramatic technique often employed by William Shakespeare was the idea of dramatic asides, where one or more characters go away from the central action to make an aside, or what are called unexpected asides. Because the audience did not know they were coming.

A fifth technique used in classical drama is sometimes called the reversal of fortune, in which the consequences of the action in a drama put the tragic figure in a position where he suddenly realizes his current situation is the exact opposite of what he thought it to be. The moment when King Oedipus realizes that he has killed his father and married his mother is a fine example of this dramatic technique.

Finaly, dramatic irony is a fifth dramatic technique often employed by the bard in his classical dramas. The idea occurs when the plot seems to lean in a certain direction and then often very quickly, it ironically goes in the opposite direction. In Sophocles' *Oedipus the King*, for example, he desires to rid the city of the plague when in reality he is the source of the disease. In Shakespeare's *Macbeth* the bard uses the technique of a dramatic apparition and where Macbeth is killed because of his lack of understanding. The theme of greed is another part of Macbeth's reversal of fortune.

Dramatic Techniques in Stephen Vicchio's Other Plays

In all four of my plays, I have made substantial use of playing with the traditional elements of classical drama. In an *Unnamed Play* written in my senior year of college, I suggested for example, that it "was not a title but merely an explanation." In the end of that drama, we find out ironically that all the male characters were women, and all the female characters are men.

In *Ivan and Adolf*, my second play. I played with the ideas of time and place, as well as the notion of what counts as a tragic figure. I also incorporated the idea from Sartre's *No Exit*, that hell is other people, in that Ivan and Adolf are Hell for each other, specifically when we understand that Adolf believes that Ivan is Jewish, while the Russian believes that Hitler is the greatest murderer of all time.

In *Executioner's Hell* I again played with the notions of time and place by incorporating an old wife's tale that the blood on the executioner's blade had healing properties, when we find out in the end of the drama this is not true. The play also mixes historical records with classical elements of drama for a tragic effect. In *Executioner' Hill*, then, we also see the technique of the reversal of fortune in the dramatic action.

Dramatic Techniques in "Hannah and Martin."

Of all of my plays, I deviated from classical dramatic technique and themes more often in *Hannah and Martin* than in my other plays. I use Hannah as a narrator to introduce the action in main scenes. I moved her around the theater in various locations to deliver her interludes. I also incorporate many of the philosophical themes that have been shared by Hannah and Martin. I also have added new historical information that comes from eye-witness testimony in Rome from September of 1945, a German-speaking Italian cousin and an Italian bell boy at the San Remo Hotel.

I have also employed the ideas of extended monologues, recurrent imagery, and even dramatic asides in *Hannah and Martin*, again chiefly through Hannah's interludes and the two Italian characters at the close of the drama. And I have adjusted the idea of time in the play, where the scenes move backwards and forwards in the drama. I have also incorporated an important ethical element in *Hannah and Martin* that is first introduced in the opening scene when Hannah informs the audience members that they will have a moral task to perform in the denouement of the play. That is, whether Hannah did the proper moral thing in forgiving her mentor Martin for joining the Nazi Party. In my notes on the play, I have even speculated about why none of the audience leaves his or her seat at the ending of the drama. This issue is bound up with the area of philosophy known as ethics, or moral theory.

In the beginning of *Hannah and Martin*, she raises some questions from the realm of what philosophers call ontology, or the study of being, when she asks if Othello really did kill Desdemona, while also raising the issue of the difference between reality and what is not real.

In short, then, I have employed some traditional Classical dramatic techniques, I have also used some of Shakespeare's additions to Classical drama, while I have also used other tricks and techniques clearly to express the ideas in *Hannah and Martin*. The play has many of the philosophical themes I have devoted my academic career to my contemplations, questions about suffering and forgiveness, evil and the nature of moral goodness, as well as the idea how to understand the idea of full moral responsibility, as a notion acquired from ancient Greek philosopher Aristotle's *Nicomachean Ethics*.

Appendix C:
An Essay on Grace, Forgiveness, and Creativity in the Plays of Stephen J. Vicchio

Be gracious to me, o Lord for to you I cry out all the day long and every day.

Psalm 86:3.

But Noah found grace in the eyes of the Lord.

Genesis 6:8.

For the Lord has given through Moses grace and truth came through Jesus Christ.

Gospel of John 1:17.

Introduction

One final aspects in all four of my dramas are the roles played by creativity and grace in my plays. In

Ivan and Adolf I suggest that goodness is a creative act because it comes from the grace of God. In contemporary times, we think of grace as "unmerited favor," in that it comes from God, and we have done nothing to deserve it.

I also suggests in material about writing *Ivan and Adolf*, that the thoughts and words of Ivan came naturally, those of Adolf more difficult, but the words of Sophie, or God, were the most laborious of all, because the character is omniscient or all-knowing, and I the playwright is only a mere mortal.

In the old Catholic Catechism, with which I grew up with in my Catholic grade school, we were taught that there are two different varieties of grace, sanctifying grace and actual grace. The former is a stable and supernatural gift that perfects the human soul in the pursuit of salvation. actual grace, on the other hand, is God's push or encouragement. It is not a permanent state. It is a nudge, most times, to do the Good.

From my perspective as a dramatist, I always have understood creativity in the words of my characters to have come as a by-product of actual grace. It is only given by God as a temporary grace or favor, if you will, to allow the person genuinely to do the moral good by the grace of God.

The ancient Hebrew word for grace is *chen*. It is made up of the letters *chet,* which looks like a fence, and *nun*, which resembles a seed of life and later in history it looked like a fish. So the Hebrew account of the word *chen* means "to separate from the outside in protecting life.

Not surprisingly, the New Testament word for grace is *charis*. It means both "grace" and "kindness." The Koine Greek term *charis* is also the origin of the English word "charity," another phenomenon that might be called "unmerited favor" from God.

It is of some importance, I believe, that *chen* in Hebrew is a masculine noun, while the noun *charis* is in the feminine. This may well be the case because God thought to bring the possibilities of grace and creativity to all of his human creatures, male and female.

Similarly, God also imbeds in the heart of every human the two *yetzerim*, or "imaginations" or "inclinations," one to good and the other to evil. Hebrew history tells us that God made the *yetzer tov*, or good inclination much stronger than the *yetzer ha ra*, or evil imagination. This may well have something to do with why no one stands up in the final scene of *Hannah and Martin*. To do so would have gone against their nature.

But it is also the case that sometimes God allows some of his creatures to be ruled by the *yetzer ha ra*, or evil imagination. These are not completely evil people, but in general the evil inclination often does the ruling of the soul in these people.

In that regard, it is interesting how many very evil people lack creativity, including Adolf Hitler and his subordinate Adolf Eichmann. In fact, in

Eichmann in Jerusalem, Dr. Arendt argued that the simplest way to describe Eichmann is that he was "too ordinary," in following orders for most of his adult life.

All of this, of course, is related to the role that forgiveness plays in all of my plays and its relationship to creativity and to the grace of God. Hitler and Eichmann were incapable to be ruled by the *yetzer tov*. Nor is this German pair of the Third Reich leadership capable of doing the moral good consistently because, among other reasons, God did not bestow upon them the grace of creativity. Thus, neither man could forgive because neither man was given the proper grace to think and act on forgiveness.

Forgiveness is a creative act. It is the opposite of revenge. Hitler and Eichmann were ruled by revenge, revenge against the Jews. If one possesses revenge the grace of forgiveness, through creativity, is nearly impossible in any human being.

Both Ivan and Adolf in the drama by that name, both men act out of the feeling of revenge, Ivan against the Russian establishment of his day, Adolf against the Jewish people and his perception and meaning of the supposed "Chosen People." Because of the strength of the revenge by which they are both ruled neither man is capable of consistently doing the moral good, for both men lack the creativity required to do it, that only comes through the actual grace of God.

In *Hannah and Martin*, on the other hand, she

clearly received the grace necessary to forgive. In her case, that grace, and thus, that creativity, was bestowed upon her by God in a night spent with Martin together on the eleventh floor of the San Remo Hotel in Rome in the summer of 1945.

Appendix D:
A Philosophical Essay on Human Nature

God and the Devil are fighting there and the battlefield is the hearts of human beings.
—Fyodor Dostoyevski. *The Brothers Karamazov.*

I still believe in spite of everything, that people are truly good at heart.
—Anne Frank. *Diary. [July 15, 1944.]*

Introduction

In regard to the philosophical views on basic human nature, we find in human literature three separate points of view. That is:

    I.   That humans are born basically or inherently, good.

II. That humans are born intrinsically evil.
III. That humans are born inherently with a mixture of good and evil.

In "Hannah and Martin" we have sketched out some of the proponents of these three positions. As we have indicated, the Hebrew Bible or Old Testament's view of a belief in two basic *yetzerim*, or inclinations or imaginations, the *yetzer ha ra*, or "evil imagination," and the *yetzer tov*, or "good inclination," is perhaps the earliest embodiment of philosophical position three introduced above.

A similar view also can be seen in certain Chinese philosophers, as we shall see later in this essay. We also will see our other two views on human nature as philosophical positions on what the ancient Chinese referred to as *xing*, which refers to the way that people were born. In fact, later in this essay, we will introduce Chinese representations of all three of our philosophical views on *xing*.

In the Western world, from the Greeks on, we also see proponents of our three theories on human nature. Socrates and Plato, for examples, were proponents of theory one; that humans are born inherently good. Aristotle, on the other hand, disagreed with his mentor Plato and held a position he called the "Golden Mean," which was the Greeks' version of theory three, that humans are born with a mixture of good and evil.

In the Medieval and Modern philosophical eras,

we see the debate on human nature continued in the West. Augustine of Hippo was an advocate of theory three, as we can see in his pronouncements that "humans are made good in Genesis," as well as the view in Augustine's *Confessions* and the *City of God*, that humans inherited from Adam and Eve what the North African bishop referred to as *Peccatum Originale*, or "Original Sin." Thus, we should put Augustine of Hippo among the advocates of theory three.

The thirteenth century, Italian philosopher, Thomas Aquinas also held a similar view in his *Summa Theologica* and *Summa Contra Gentiles.* He also completed a work that he called *De Malo*, or *On Evil*. In this work, Aquinas adopted Augustine's view that evil is not something real, it is merely an absence of the good, or a *Privatio Boni.*

In more modern times, the figures of Thomas Hobbes and Jean-Jacque Rousseau took up the problem at the heart of this essay. As we shall see, they are proponents of theory one and theory two introduced in this introduction. We will divide this essay into the following parts. In the first of these we will speak of what Chinese philosophy has contributed to the issue of human nature. In the second section, we will say more about the disagreement between Thomas Hobbes and Jean-Jacque Rousseau; and in the third and final section, we will make some observations on what Hannah Arendt and Martin Heidegger had to write and say about basic human nature.

Human Nature and Chinese Philosophy

In Ancient Chinese philosophy we find representatives of all three of our views on human nature, or what the Chinese call *xing*, or "basic human nature." In his famous *Analects*, Kong Qiu, also known as Confucius, in book seventeen of that work Confucius speaks of *xing*.

In that section, Confucius speaks of *xing* and his belief that humans are born good, or theory number one in this essay. This same theory was advocated by Chinese philosopher, Mencius [fourth century BCE.]. Mencius is best known for his theory called *Xing Shan*, or the notion that human nature is basically good.

Zhu Xi (1130–1200) built upon Mencius' theory of natural goodness, while also giving some small modifications to the theory. Zhu Xi believed that human beings are naturally good, but desires for evil arise later in life.

The notion that human beings are inherently evil also can be seen in Ancient Chinese philosophy in the work of Xunzi, or Hsun Tzu (310–220 BCE.). In short, Xunzi held a philosophical view on *xing* that humans by their very nature are evil. Xunzi returned to this view in many places of his major works such as the *Xunzi*.

Finally, our theory number three that humans are born with both the inherent capacity to do evil, as well as the intrinsic capacity to do evil can be seen in the philosophical views of Wang Yangming (1472–1529.). Wang developed the idea of what he called "innate knowing," in which he argues that every person from birth knows the difference between good and evil. Wang thought that this knowledge is intuitive and not rational, and thus inherently and intuitively known.

Wang Yangming's work was a great influence on many modern Japanese philosophers, like Mootori Norinaga (1730–1809). In fact, Norinaga's school is known as the Wang School. Wang's philosophy celebrated the innate goodness of human nature while at the same time he also emphasized his belief that evil is also inherently known.

His ideas continue to emphasize Chinese thought, as well as Chinese scholars around the world. In summary, then, we find in the history of Chinese, philosophical thought the views that humans are born basically good, that humans are basically evil, and in Wang Yangming's thought that humans inherently know both good and evil.

Human Nature in Modern Philosophy: Hobbes, Rousseau, and Locke.

The question of basic human nature continued in the Early Modern period of Western philosophy in the philosophical figures of Thomas Hobbes (1588–1659), Jean-Jacques Rousseau (1712–1778) and English philosopher, John Locke (1632–1704.) We have chosen these particular philosophers because they represent three different views concerning basic human nature.

Thomas Hobbes was a Materialist (one who believes that only matter exists) and he rejected Dualism (one who believes that both matter and soul or spirit exist.) Hobbes argued that the idea of a human, immaterial soul made no sense. Thus, human nature—in his view—was decidedly a materialistic problem.

Thomas Hobbes' most important claim about basic human nature is that it is inherently Evil. He makes this claim in his most important work, the *Leviathan*, written and published in 1651, as well as secondary works he called *Human Nature* (1650) and *On Man*, published in 1658, one of his final philosophical works.

Hobbes' pessimistic view of human nature was contrasted with the positions of Jean-Jacques Rousseau and John Locke on the same philosophical problem. In his major work, *On the Origins of Inequality*, Rousseau makes the claim that human beings are inherently morally Good, as opposed to Hobbes' understanding that humans are intrinsically evil.

For Rousseau there are three separate aspects of his theory of human nature. These may be summarized in the following way:

1. The conception that human beings are animals.
2. Human nature is what all humans share in common.
3. What is innate, or in-born, as opposed to acquired.

From these three aspects, Rousseau arrived at the conclusion that human beings are inherently good, the opposite of Thomas Hobbes' perspective. From these two philosophers, one English and one Swiss, then, we see the first two theories we have sketched out in the introduction of this essay. Rousseau believed in theory one, while Hobbes was an advocate of theory two.

These two philosophical positions on basic human nature in Western modern philosophy are quite different from a third perspective we find in the philosophical work on human nature of British philosopher, John Locke. Like Aristotle, Locke was an Empiricist, that all knowledge comes from the use of the senses.

A central idea of Lockean thought was the notion of what he called the *tabula rasa*, or "blank slate." Locke thought that all humans are born with a barren, empty, malleable mind. Every aspect of one's character is something observed, perceived, and learned through the senses.

John Locke also rejected theory number three in that if theories one and two are discarded, then theory three—which is made up of one and two—must be rejected, as well.

With his idea of the tabula rasa, it should be clear that John Locke rejected both theories one and two of the introduction to this essay, and ultimately argued for the fourth position, in which the human innately acts like a sponge, or blank slate on which is written all of one's experiences.

Each of these four philosophical views on innate human nature are also tied to what was called in the Early Modern period the "state of nature," or what humans were like before there were any human collectives. Hobbes' view of the state of nature, not surprisingly, was pessimistic, while that of Jean-Jacque Rousseau was optimistic.

In his *Two Treatises on Government*, Locke argues that ether than nature be optimistic or pessimistic, people were thought to be born with natural rights, such as freedom, equality, and independence. For Locke, the major moral responsibility in the state of nature is to respect each other's rights. Thus, Locke's view of the state of nature is intrinsically tied to his notion of the *tabula rasa*.

In John Locke's view, he makes three major points about human nature. First, the state of nature was characterized by the absence of government but not by the absence of mutual cooperation. Second, that the mind is a *tabula rasa* at birth and finally, people are naturally cooperative and reasonable. In summary, then, Locke's view on human nature emphasized human rights, reason, and the potential for cooperation.

Contemporary Views of Human Nature: John Rawls, Robert Nozick, and the Nature-Nurture Conflict

As we have seen, the notion of a state of nature, either real or hypothetical, was most influential in the seventeenth and eighteenth centuries. Nevertheless, it has also influenced more recent attempts to establish objective norms of justice and fairness, notably two American philosophers, John Rawls and Robert Nozick. The former in his book, *A Theory of Justice*, published in 1971, and the latter in Nozick's *Anarchy, State and Utopia* (1974.)

Rawls' view of the state of nature and Justice consists of three separate notions. He labels these:

I. The Principle of Equality.
II. The Principle of Difference.
III. The Veil of Ignorance

Under the principle of equality, Rawls argues that human beings are born with certain natural rights, such as life, liberty, and the pursuit of happiness. But sometimes those individual or group rights conflict with each other, and here the principle of difference comes into play. Rawls says if you want to limit or cancel some natural rights one has to show that two things are true. First, that it is good for society as a whole, and secondly, that must include society's least advantaged members.

Now Rawls believed if one applies these two principles of justice or fairness to a given moral question, one should be able to derive an answer from the two principles. And this moral answer derived from the two principles should be the same response derived from the application of Rawls' "veil of ignorance."

The veil of ignorance in Rawls' view involves the application of three steps. These are the following:

> I. Identify all the players in the moral situation.
> II. Imagine you are one of the players but not which one.
> III. Under those two conditions, what would you want the decision-maker to do in that moral situation?

Rawls believed that the same moral answer one derived from the principles of equality and difference should also be the same moral decision derived from the application of his veil of ignorance. Rawls believed that human beings inherently possess certain natural rights and if these rights are limited or canceled, that must be good for society and its least advantaged members.

Three years after the publication of Rawls' *Theory of Justice*, another American philosopher named Robert Nozick, in his book, *Anarchy, State, and Utopia* also turned to the idea of a hypothetical state. He does this by speaking about what he calls "libertarian rights," attempting to show that only a minimal state can arise via an "invisible hand" process out of the state of nature without violating the rights of individuals. Nozick argued against Rawls theory of justice for many reasons, but the chief of these is Rawls argued for more than a minimal state.

A second idea of substance we see in Robert Nozick's political philosophy is the distinction between positive and negative rights. Positive rights, also called freedoms to, include those rights guaranteed by the U.S. Constitution. Negative rights, or freedoms from, are those things that all rational people want to avoid such as suffering and death.

FREEDOMS TO	FREEDOMS FROM
life, liberty, pursuit of happiness, free speech, freedom of assembly	suffering, death, conflict, deception, dishonesty, etc

Hannah and Martin on Human Nature

Most of the major comments that Hannah Arendt made about basic human nature came in her 1958 work, *The Human Condition*. In this text, Arendt proports to give an account of what she calls "human activities" and how they should be and have been understood throughout Western philosophy.

Arendt opens the book with a distinction between what she calls the *vita activa*, or "active life," and the *vita contemplative*, or the "contemplative life." The *Human Condition* was first published in 1958, and a second edition, with an introduction by Margaret Canovan, was published in 1998. It consists of a prologue and six separate parts. These six separate parts may be summarized this way:

      I.   The Human Condition.
      II.   The Public and Private Realms.
      III. Labor.
      IV. Work.
      V.   Action.
      VI. The *Vita Activa* and the Modern Age.

Professor Arendt points out that the Ancient Greek philosophers put more emphasis on the contemplative life. She says that Karl Marx flipped the hierarchy, claiming that the contemplative life is merely a superstructure on the fundamental basic life processes of a society. Hannah Arendt's thesis, on the other hand, is that the *vita activa* is neither superior, nor inferior to the contemplative life, nor are they identical.

Arendt goes on in the *Human Condition,* or "active life" that the vita active consists of three different kinds of activities, labor, work, and action. Early in the *Human Condition*, Dr. Arendt made a distinction between what she called the "public" and "private" realms. She tells us in Section II of the book that ancient Greek life was divided between these two realms. The public realm is where social actions take place. The private realm takes place in the household ruled by its head. The mark of the private realm is not intimacy, as it is in modern times, but rather it is biological necessity. In the private realm, the heads of households took care of the needs for food, clothing, shelter, and even sexual activity.

Arendt points out that if the head of a household is unable to supply these biological necessities, one was not free of them and also could not participate in the public realm as a free person/citizen. Hannah Arendt goes on in Section II of the book that the head of the family among the ancient Greeks often relegated the private realm to his wife, but the public realm for the Greeks was accorded a higher status than the private realm.

In the same section of the *Human Condition*, Arendt goes on to tell us that with the fall of the Roman Empire, the Christian Church took over the control of the public realm. Arendt views the public realm in early Christianity. The modern period saw the rise of a third realm that she calls the "social realm".

In Sections III and IV of the *Human Condition*, Hannah Arendt first made her distinction between labor and work. In her view, work, as opposed to labor, has a clearly defined beginning and end. It leaves behind something durable such as a tool rather than an object for consumption. These durable objects become a part of the world.

Arendt also believed that in the Modern period of history we began to see a third realm of human life. She calls this the "social realm." This realm is concerned with providing the biological needs, but it does so at the level of the state. For Arendt, this was the beginning of social welfare programs.

In Section V of the *Human Condition*, Hannah Arendt sketches out her understanding of the realm of action that has two primary aspects, freedom and distinction. She also placed speech and action in the realm of action. This realm also includes stories or narratives from the point of view of the person acting. These stories are recorded in documents, moments, which tell us more about the subject of the narrative. For Hannah Arendt, these stories or narratives become the sum total of the human self.

Over and against this view of the self in the *Human Condition* is Arendt's background in the philosophy of Augustine of Hippo. Indeed, she wrote her Ph.D. dissertation on the North African, Christian Bishop. The dissertation was entitled *Der Liebesbegriff bei Augustin. Versuch einer philosophischen Interpretation* or *On the concept of love in the thought of Saint Augustine: Attempt at a philosophical interpretation*, also known as *Love and Saint Augustine*. In this work, written in 1928 and published a year later, Arendt makes distinctions among three different varieties of love—love as craving or desire; love in relation to God; and what she calls *caritas*, or "neighborly love," the most fundamental of the three.

Dr. Arendt tied brotherly love to the second of

the great commandments, or golden rule. That is, love thy neighbor as thyself. This view of love, in Hannah Arendt's understanding is far more important than the other two.

Martin Heidegger, on the other hand, wrote very little about what we would call the Classic problem of basic human nature. The places where he does discuss the phenomenon are to be found in his classic work, *Being and Time*. In that work, Heidegger defines *dasein,* or human existence, as "a living thing that has *logos*", one of the Ancient Greek terms for reason.

Following Aristotle's structure of the great chain of being that catalogues all living things according to the parts of the soul, humans are above the animals and plants because humans have reason that is not associated with the other two, lower members of the great chain of being. Aristotle's great chain of being looks something like this:

> God [Reason]
> Humans [Reason, Spirit and Vegetative]
> Animals [Spirit and Vegetative]
> Plants [Vegetative]

In the thirteenth century, Thomas Aquinas noticed that something was missing in the great chain of being, and that was "Angels who have reason and spirit but are without the vegetative because they do not have physical bodies. Thus, the chain should be God, angels, humans, animals, and plants.

In *Being and Time*, Heidegger describes *logos* as" pre-language," a preliminary perception of the world which often finds expression in verbal communication. This view is made clear by Heidegger's account of speaking in which "formless, prior understanding" or *logos*, "is shaped into verbal expression." Nevertheless, for Martin Heidegger what sets humans apart from the rest of the world's creatures, as he borrowed from Aristotle, is nothing more than reason itself.

Appendix E:
More On Plato's Eternal Forms

And the greatest of these forms is the Good, represented by the Sun.
—Plato. *Phaedo.*

Earlier in this drama, we made references to Plato's Theory of the Eternal Forms and their relationships to his allegory of the cave, and the parts of the human soul from the Greek's perspective. His theory of the Eternal Forms suggests that the physical world, the world of the senses, is not as fundamentally real as the eternal forms, or *Eidos* in Classical Greek. For Plato, these forms are non-physical, timeless, absolute and un-changing. Objects and ideas in the physical world are mere "imitations" of the Eternal Forms.

The word *Eidos* has a Sanskrit root. It is related to other words like *morphe*, or "shape," and *phenomenon*, or "appearance." The notion of Forms began with the pre-Socratics, beginning with Thales who noticed that appearances change, so he began to ponder what change really is. Plato answered that question by relating that the physical world is not the most real realm of existence, but rather imitations of the Eternal Forms.

All of this is borne out by Plato's allegory of the cave. The objects that move on the platform represent the physical world and the shadows on the wall are mere imitations of those objects. When the prisoner gets free and ascends the stairs, leaving the cave, he discovers the Sun, a representation of the highest of the Forms, the good.

When the escaped prisoner returns to the cave, he begins to tell his colleagues what he has found, the existence of the Sun as well as another level of reality. that goes beyond the mere physical realm of objects and ideas and gives some hints of this greater level of reality, the Eternal Forms, to his friends.

Plato's metaphor for the human soul—with the chariot, the charioteer, and the two horses—is also tied to these other Platonic ideas. He tells us in the *Phaedo*, as well as in the *Republic,* that the rational part of the soul is able to apprehend the Eternal Forms and stands for Reason, the Charioteer. The darker horse stands for the emotions and passion, what Plato refers to as the "appetitive" part of the soul. The lighter horse is the spirited element of the soul, the rules of society.

For Plato, every object, idea, or quality in the physical world—dogs, humans, mountains, courage, love, and the good, has a Form that answers the question, "What is that?", or "Why is this thing and that thing the same thing?", such as pointing to two triangles. Plato's answer to that question is that they are both imitations of the Eternal Form of the triangle.

Plato's theory of the Forms gave rise to what is known as the problem of universals in the history of Western philosophy. Plato would say that both of our objects are triangles because they both imitate the Eternal Form of the triangle.

Plato's student, Aristotle, would answer the same question by saying that both objects have the necessary and sufficient conditions for calling something a triangle. These are:

    I.   A three-sided geometric figure.
    II.   With three sides
    III. Whose angles are equal to 180 degrees.

For Plato, why are my eyes, my jeans and the sky blue? Because they participate in the Eternal Form of blueness. And it is only the rational part of the soul that is able to comprehend these connections.

In "Hannah and Martin" these Platonic issues appear several times in the play. These may be found at Act I, Scenes 2, 3, 5, and 6 and Act II, Scenes 2 and 3.

Hannah Arendt knew her Plato very well and first read him, in the original Greek, at the Gymnasium, the German equivalent of high school.

She first read Plato in the Benjamin Jowett translation from Greek to German in the early 1920s and then into English in the 1950s and 1960s. Hannah's Ph.D. dissertation on the three kinds of love in Saint Augustine of Hippo is also related to many of the ideas we have introduced here. In fact, the most important philosophical source, in addition to the Bible, for the North African Bishop was the writing of the great Athenian philosopher, Plato.

Appendix F: Thoughts on Aristotle's Ethics

The most thought-provoking thing in our thought-provoking time is that we still are not thinking.
—Martin Heidegger. *Being and Time.*

The ideal subject of totalitarianism that the convinced Nazi or the dedicated Communist, but people for whom the distinction between fact and fiction, or true and false, no longer exists.
—Hannah Arendt, *Totalitarianisms.*

Be a free thinker and don't accept everything you hear as truth. Be critical and evaluate what you believe in.
—Aristotle. *Ethics.*

Introduction

Over the course of this work we have mentioned three separate ideas related to the thought of the Athenian thinker, Aristotle. (384-322 B.C.) These ideas are the great chain of being, the nature of moral responsibility, and virtue and the moral good. This appendix will unfold with three separate sections on each of these ideas.

Each of these three ideas appear in the carrying out of the drama of *Hannah and Martin*. We mention them here by providing information about how these notions of Aristotle may be understood.

The Great Chain of Being

The idea of the "great chain of being" can be found in Aristotle's *Metaphysics*, where he posits that all living things can be seen as existing in a great chain of being, depending on the number of functions of the soul a being possesses. At the bottom of the chain are plants that only possess a vegetative function of the soul.

Above them are animals who possess the vegetative and the sensitive functions of the soul. Above animals are human beings who have the vegetative, the sensitive, and the rational functions of the soul.

Above humans in Aristotle's scheme is God that he defines as an "unmoved mover," or "first cause". For Aristotle, God is pure reason or what he defines as "The thought that thinks itself." God does not have the sensitive and vegetative functions of the soul because He does not feel emotions and He has no body, so He has no vegetative function. Thus, for Aristotle, the great chain of being looks like this:

> God, or *Theos* [Pure Reason]
>
> Humans, or *Anthropoi* [Vegetative, sensitive and rational]
>
> Animals, or *Zoo* [Vegetative and sensitive]
>
> Plants, or *Phyto* [The Vegetative function of the soul]

In the 13th century, Italian philosopher, Thomas Aquinas thought something was missing from the great chain of being, a being who possesses the rational and sensitive functions but not the vegetative because this being has no physical body. This being is angels. So, Thomas added angels to the great chain of being. In his scheme we now have this:

> God [*Deus*]
>
> Angels [*Angeli*]
>
> Humans [*Homines*]
>
> Animals [*Animale*]
>
> Plants [*Plante*]

Thomas also points out the symmetry of this new scheme. in terms of functions of the soul. Thus we get

God [Only Rational]

Angels [Rational and Sensitive]

Humans [Rational, Sensitive, and Vegetative]

Animals [Sensitive and Vegetative]

Plants [Only Vegetative]

Thus, the symmetry in terms of soul functions goes: 1,2, 3, 2, 1.

Aristotle on Moral Responsibility

In Books V and VI of his *Ethics*, Aristotle sketches out his view of the notion of moral Responsibility. In those passages the Greek philosopher points out that in order to be fully morally responsible for an action, that person must meet four conditions. These are expressed this way in Book V:

    I.   First, the intention to do moral right or moral wrong.

    II.   Second, one must know what moral right and moral wrong are.

    III.   Third, one must have knowledge of the circumstances under which the action occurs.

    IV.   Fourth, and finally, one must have possessed the "ability to do otherwise."

By this fourth condition, Aristotle says that the person must act freely and "without internal or externa constraint. By external constraint Aristotle means no one is holding a gun to his head or knife to his throat or similar circumstances of that kind. By internal constraint, Aristotle meant that the actor does not possess a mental disease or defect that could be a cause of the behavior in question.

Aristotle also suggests there are degrees of moral responsibility from fully responsible to minor or even shared responsibility. Aristotle recommends the application of what he calls the "But For" clause that essentially says "But for the action of A, X would not have happened, Thus in a contract murder where A hires B to kill C, A and B are both fully responsible. For Aristotle the key question is this: But for the actions of A and B, person C would still be alive.

Interestingly enough, we know that Aristotle was correct about full moral responsibility because we still employ his formulation in contemporary times. Consider the four most popular excuses that people employ in order to avoid moral responsibility. These are:

I. I did not mean to do it. [no intention]

V. I did not know it was wrong. [no knowledge of moral wrong.]

VI. I did not know it was happening. [no knowledge of the circumstances.]

VII. There is nothing else I could have done. [no ability to do otherwise.]

The Nature of Moral Virtue and moral Goodness

The third and final element of the Ethics of Aristotle is the natures of moral virtue and goodness. His best account of Virtue is in Books V to VII of his *Ethics*. There the Greek philosopher define a Virtue as "a mean between two extremes." Thus, the virtue called courage is a mean between two extremes. He called these extreme bravery and recklessness. Thus Courage is a mean between these two things, one a deficiency of fear and the other an abundance of Fear. Aristotle makes the same kind of judgments about other moral virtues, or what are called "cardinal virtues". These are: as well. These are:

> Prudence, or practical wisdom.
>
> Justice, or getting what one is due.
>
> Temperance, or moderation.

Like Aristotle's view of courage, these other cardinal virtues are each a mean between two extremes, a deficiency and an abundance. Thus, the star student of Plato's tells us that the cardinal virtues and their deficiencies and abundances look like this:

Recklessness	**Courage**	**Bravery**
Injustice	Justice	Over justice
Not enough pleasure	Temperance	Too much pleasure
Over indulging	Prudence	Under indulging

The Classical names Aristotle gives to these cardinal virtues are the following:

Courage [*Andreia*]
Justice [*Dikaiosyne*]
Temperance. [*Sophrosyne*]
Prudence [*Phronesis*]

Aristotle also tells us that the subtotal of practicing these cardinal virtues is what he calls the good life or *eudaimonia*, Aristotle's word for "human happiness." Another important point he makes about moral virtues is that the individual possession is subordinate to the collective virtue, that is the state. In this regard, Aristotle also suggests that states and nations may be judged by the collective moral virtues they display. In that sense, some states or nations are more morally good than others.

This, of course, raises the question about what moral virtues are displayed by China, Russia, Iran, Israel, and the United States, where freedom and equality have been replaced by equity, diversity, and inclusion.

Appendix G:
Love in Saint Augustine

To fall in love is the greatest romance, to seek Him the greatest adventure, to find Him the greatest achievement.
   —Saint Augustine. "Sermon on Love."

In order to discover the character of people we have only to observe what they love.
   —Saint Augustine. "Sermon on Love."

My love for Linton is like the foliage in the woods, time will change it. I am well aware as winter changes the trees. My love for Heathcliffe resembles eternal rocks beneath a source of little delight Nelly, I love Heathcliffe. This stormy passion is not mere saccharine, literary sentimentality."
   —Emily Bronte. *Wuthering Heights*

Introduction

The purpose of this appendix is to make some comments about what Saint Augustine, the Bishop of Hippo (354-430) believed about the concept of love. He wrote and spoke about love in many places, most especially in his two major works, *The Confessions* Book X and *The City of God* Book XIX, but also in a works that came to be called his "Sermon on Love," which came as part of a commentary on 1 John.

This appendix is important because Hannah Arendt's Ph.D. thesis is on the varieties of love in Saint Augustine, under the direction of Karl Jaspers at the University of Heidelberg in late 1928.

From Martin Heidegger, Arendt learned that Augustine referred to three separate kinds of love, the subject-matter of this appendix. These three varieties of Love that we find in Arendt's thesis and in Augustine's "Sermon on Love" are precisely the same. They both call these: love of the appetites, love of God, and brotherly love. The Medieval Latin of Augustine and Thomas Aquinas had three separate nouns for love. These were: *amor*, *caritas*, and *dilectio*. The corresponding verbs of the first two are *amare* and *diligere*.

The three varieties of Love that we find in Saint Augustine's "Sermon on Love" and in Arendt's Ph.D. thesis are precisely the same. They both call these the love of appetites, the love of God, and brotherly love. Medieval Latin had three had three separate nouns for love. These were *amor*, *dilectio*, and *caritas*. The corresponding verbs for the first two of these were *amare* and *deligere*

Two other ideas about Love are significant in understanding Arendt's views on the matter. She called these *natalitat*, or natality, and *amore mundi* or love of the world. Natality, of course, refers to being born into the world, a necessary condition in Heidegger view of being. One place where Dr. Arendt spoke extensively on love of the world is in her *denktagebuch*, or thinking journal.

In that journal Dr. Arendt related that love of the world is the practice of understanding and reconciling one's self with the world and comes to terms with what really happened. As she puts it, "It is the idea that if we are to face the world and come to terms of what really happened and what is happening today. How can we live in a world where something like the Holocaust is possible?"

In fact, in a letter to Karl Jaspers from August 5, 1955, she told her thesis advisor that she had originally planned to entitle her thesis, "The Love of the World," but by 1929, she had changed her mind about the matter.

Appendix H:
Foreign Words and Phrases

In the course of this drama, I have used many foreign words and phrases, including seven languages other than English. These were Chinese, Classical Hebrew, Classical Greek, German, Medieval Latin, Modern Hebrew, and Spanish. I have transliterated each of these foreign words and phrases and then put them in alphabetical order. These are the following:

Term	Meaning	Origin
Ahavat Yisrael	Love for the Jews	Modern Hebrew
Aionis	Eternal	Classical Greek
Amare	To love	Medieval Latin
Amor	Love	Medieval Latin
Amor appetitus	Love of appetites	Medieval Latin
Amor Creator	Love of God	Medieval Latin
Amor mundi	Love of the world	Medieval Latin

Andreia	Courage	Classic Greek
Angeli	Angel	Medieval Latin
Animale	Animal	Medieval Latin
Anthropoi	Human	Classic Greek
Banal	Hopelessly flawed	German
Caritas	Neighborly love	Medieval Latin
Charis	Charity, grace, kindness	Classical Greek
Chen	Grace, to separate from the outside in protecting life	Classical Hebrew
Dasein	Human Existence	German
Der Liebesbegriff bei Augustin. Versuch einer philosophischen Interpretation	On the concept of love in the thought of Saint Augustine: Attempt at a philosophical interpretation	German
Deus	God	Medieval Latin
Denktagebuch	Thought diary	German
Dikaiosyne	Justice	Classic Greek
Dilecto	Beloved	Medieval Latin
Dilecto proximi	Beloved neighbor, or Neighborly love	Medieval Latin
Diligere	To Love	Medieval Latin
Eidos	Form	Classical Greek
Ego	Ego	German
Eros	Love	Classical Greek
Es	Id	German
Fuhrer	Premiere Leader	German

Goldene regel	Golden rule	German
Homines	Humans	Medieval Latin
Ich habe schon sehr fruh in Jahre 1924 geahnt	I suspected it very early on sometime in 1924	German
Ich sehe Herr Schmidt dass asie sie Abschnitte 246 to 250, sehr grundlich gelesen haben	I see Mr. Schmidt that you have read sections 246 to 250 very thoroughly.	German
Ifantile neurose	Infantile neurosi	German
Logos	Reason	Classical Greek
Mantis	Seer	Classical Greek
Morphe	Shape	Classical Greek
Natalitat	Natality	German
Nimm meine medizing	Take my medicine	German
Ontos	To be	Classical Greek
Peccatum Originale	Original Sin	Medieval Latin
Phaedo	On The Soul, a work by Plato	Classical Greek
Phaedrus	A work by Plato	Classical Greek
Phenomenon	Appearance	Classical Greek
Phronesis	Prudence	Classical Greek
Phyto	Plants	Classical Greek

Plante	Plants	Medieval Latin
Politeia	Republic, a work by Plato	Classical Greek
Privatio boni	Privation or an absence from the Good	Medieval Latin
Psyche	Soul	Classical Greek
Schatten und fake level	Shadows and fake level	German
Schon fur dich	Good for you	German
Schwarzes Notizbuch	Black Notebook	German
Sein und Zeit	Being and Time	German
Sophos	Wisdom	Classical Greek
Sophrosyne	Temperance	Classical Greek
Superwego	Superego	German
Symposia	Drinking party, a work of Plato	Classical Greek
Tabula Rasa	Blank Slate	Medieval Latin
Tempus fugit	Time flies	Medieval Latin
Theos	God	Classical Greek
Un momentito Senor	May I have a moment, Sir	Spanish
Vita activa	Active life	Medieval Latin
Vita contemplative	Contemplative life	Medieval Latin
Wann wussten Sie dass ich judin bin	When did you know that I was Jewish	German

Welfjudentum	World Jewry	German
Xing	Basic human nature	Chinese
Xing Shan	Good human nature	Chinese
Yetzer Ha Ra	Evil imagination or inclination	Classical Hebrew
Yetzer Tov	Good imagination or inclination	Classical Hebrew
Yetzerim	Imaginations or Inclinations	Classical Hebrew
Zoo	Animals	Classical Greek
Zugenorh-origheit	Belonging	German

In total, I have employed seventy-two foreign words and expressions. Twenty-three words are from Classical Greek, while German has twenty-one. Medieval Latin has twenty, and four are from Classical Hebrew. Two are from Chinese, and for both Modern Hebrew and Spanish I have used only one.

About the Author

Stephen J. Vicchio was born and raised in Baltimore, Maryland, in a working-class neighborhood. He was educated at the University of Maryland; Yale Divinity School; Hertford College, Oxford, and acquired a PhD from St. Andrews University in Fife, Scotland. He has authored over forty works including three other plays: *The Unnamed Play*, *Ivan and Adolf: The Last Man in Hell*, and *Executioner's Hill*.

www.ingramcontent.com/pod-product-compliance
Lightning Source LLC
Chambersburg PA
CBHW032001080426
42735CB00007B/468